freedom from my fears

freedom from my fears

40 Meditations *on* David's Psalms *and* Prayers

Harold Myra

Freedom from My Fears: 40 Meditations on David's Psalms and Prayers

Interior design by Michael J. Williams

ISBN: 978-1-64070-233-2

Library of Congress Cataloging-in-Publication Data Available

Printed in the United States of America
23 24 25 26 27 28 29 30 / 8 7 6 5 4 3 2 1

I sought the LORD, and he answered me
and delivered me from all my fears.

—David, Psalm 34:4 ESV

Contents

Welcome

It's said we now live in an age of anxiety. Vivid images show us troubles everywhere: Families fleeing wars. Devastating fires, storms, tsunamis, and earthquakes. Hatreds and cultural chaos. Our times are full of heartbreak and dire predictions.

David, the "sweet psalmist" who wrote seventy-three of the psalms, brought his fears to the Lord. Facing the fearsome giant Goliath and then decades of turmoil, he focused on God. Many of his psalms are linked to his deadly troubles . . . for instance, a murderous king hunting him into a cave (Psalm 18), a prophet accusing him of adultery and treachery (Psalm 51), and his son betraying him and inciting the nation to rise up and assassinate him (Psalm 3).

David's psalms are full of anguished cries to the Lord, yet also joyous praise. The range of his prayers is broad, from "The Lord is my shepherd" to "I am worn out from sobbing" to "Purify me from my sins, and I will be clean."

How did this "man after God's own heart" deal with his lifetime of troubles? How can we learn from his story as we ponder his crying out to God in the midst of difficulty and his praising God despite so much violence, many betrayals, and tragic failures?

Psalms has been called God's prayer book. Christians have long viewed it as training us in prayer, and David's prayers in particular, out of the cauldron of his experiences, can teach, challenge, and inspire us.

To give you context for these devotions, I've divided the book into four parts, each covering one period of David's tumultuous life. The ten meditations for each period, which include selections from David's psalms interspersed with responsive prayers for our times, explore his life and his resulting songs of praise, desperation, penitence, and divine glory.

CONSIDER

None of David's psalms speaks specifically to his triumph over Goliath.

Not once does David boast about his own abilities. He only boasts in God.

—Tim Stafford

PART ONE

The Anointed Shepherd Picks Five Stones

The story of David and Goliath, found in 1 Samuel 17, starts with a scene of men terrified. For forty days the troops of Israel's army had been trembling at the Philistine giant's shouts and taunts. No one wanted to fight nine-foot-tall Goliath brandishing a spear as big as a beam with a fifteen-pound spearhead. "I defy the armies of Israel today!" he shouted. "Send me a man who will fight me!"

No man would.

But then along came a young shepherd.

David arrived simply to deliver food for his older brothers. Shepherds were looked down on, and he was the youngest of eight. In his brothers' eyes, he was just a brash kid. Yet when David watched Goliath shouting his threats, instead of being terrified he was outraged. "Who is this pagan Philistine anyway," he demanded, "that he is allowed to defy the armies of the living God?"

Why wasn't David terrified like everyone else?

Earlier, something had happened to transform him. The prophet Samuel had come to Bethlehem where he lived. As young David stood among his older brothers, Samuel took a flask of olive oil and anointed him as the new king. The Scriptures tell us, "The Spirit of the LORD came powerfully upon David from that day on."

When King Saul on the battlefield heard about what David was saying about Goliath, he sent for him. The young man boldly volunteered to take up the giant's challenge. "Don't worry about this Philistine," David said. "I'll go fight him!" The king tried to dissuade him, but the shepherd was full of God's Spirit.

Armed only with his shepherd's staff and sling, David picked five smooth stones from a stream and put them into his bag. Then he started across the valley toward the giant.

Goliath sneered. "Am I a dog," he roared, "that you come at me with a stick?" He cursed David and threatened he'd give his flesh to animals and birds.

David responded, "You come to me with sword, spear, and javelin, but I come to you in the name of the LORD of Heaven's Armies. . . . This is the LORD's battle."

As Goliath moved to attack, David ran toward him and with his sling hurled a stone. It hit the Philistine in the forehead and he stumbled. Then he fell facedown on the ground.

David ran over, pulled Goliath's sword from its sheath, and used it to kill him and to cut off his head.

After Goliath's defeat the Israelites celebrated a great victory and David was instantly a hero. King Saul made him a commander over men of war and people sang about David's exploits in battles. Saul's son Jonathan bonded with him.

Yet the young leader had plenty of deadly troubles ahead. God had rejected Saul as king, which was why Samuel had anointed David as God's new choice. Evil spirits were tormenting Saul and he began to hate David. For what was coming next, the young hero would need as much courage and power from God's Spirit as he had in the moment he faced Goliath.

We get a glimpse of his spiritual experiences in these excerpts from David's Psalm 34, written during a time of desperation:

I will praise the Lord at all times.
  I will constantly speak his praises. . . .

I prayed to the Lord, and he answered me.
  He freed me from all my fears.

DAY 1

Staring at Goliath

1 Samuel 17:1–11

Before David volunteered to fight the giant, why hadn't one of his brothers stepped up? They were terrified by Goliath's threats. For forty days the giant had taunted them, with the Philistine army raring to start slaughtering the Israelites.

It's easy to understand why their fears kept growing day after day. The brothers' eyes were on Goliath.

Our eyes are on our screens, and it's hard to avoid our anxieties about all the threats and terrible things. We may try to think about "whatsoever things are lovely . . . [and] of good report," but we live with instant news of tragedies and malignant forces threatening to destroy all we know and love.

Few of us can insulate ourselves from vivid images of the brokenness of our world. If staring at screens is anything like staring at Goliath, how can we be like David instead of his brothers?

The lessons for us are pretty clear.

David's eyes were on God.

Jesus said, "'You must love the LORD your God with all your heart, all your soul, and all your mind.' This is the first and greatest commandment." We see throughout his seventy-three psalms that David's heart, soul, and mind were on God, sometimes exuberantly praising him, other times crying out to him in desperation.

David saw Goliath from God's perspective.

When we see the giants of injustice and hatred as hostilities against God, we remember this is why the Father sent his Son to redeem us, and we affirm that hope. The good news of redemption changes our view of brokenness and despair.

David was outraged.

We hear a lot about outrage these days, too often aimed at people on opposite sides of culture wars. It's easy to get caught up in them and harder to discern how to direct our outrage at the terrible things that grieve the heart of God. David felt righteous indignation. When we are outraged, we need to pray that our indignation is righteous because we are seeing from God's perspective and praying for his guidance.

David facing Goliath was in step with the Spirit.

We read that after Samuel anointed him, "The Spirit of the LORD came powerfully upon David from that day on." We also read in Zechariah 4 the declaration that echoes David's response to Goliath's threats: "It is not by force nor by strength, but by my Spirit, says the LORD of Heaven's Armies."

MARVELOUS THINGS

SELECTIONS FROM PSALM 9

I will praise you, LORD, with all my heart;
I will tell of all the marvelous things you have done.
I will be filled with joy because of you.
I will sing praises to your name, O Most High.

My enemies retreated;
they staggered and died when you appeared.

Lord, our dangerously wired world is full of troubles and terrible violence. Community conflicts set us against each other. And, Spirit of God, you know I am not immune! The giants of dismay, doubt, anger, and guilt threaten my sense of your presence.

Come with your grace, Lord, and pour your praises into our spirits. Grant us your joy. Bless us with your perspective. As you did for David, cause our spiritual enemies to retreat at your appearance.

We praise you for all the ways you have brought hope and light to us.

The LORD is a shelter for the oppressed,
a refuge in times of trouble.
Those who know your name trust in you,
for you, O LORD, do not abandon those
who search for you.

Lord, we do search for you, and we do trust in you. Be our shelter in the storms!

When so many paths that people take these days lead to heartache and destruction, we praise you for showing us your paths that lead to healing and wholeness.

We praise you for your amazing grace. Open our hearts to all your wonderful works.

DAY 2

Fear Not!

1 Samuel 17:31–36

When King Saul warned David that he couldn't fight the giant since he was "only a boy" and Goliath a man of war, David replied, "The LORD who rescued me from the claws of the lion and the bear will rescue me from this Philistine!"

The dramatic differences between the bold young shepherd and the terrified king illustrate the assurance we find in Isaiah 26:3: "You will keep in perfect peace all who trust in you, all whose thoughts are fixed on you!" David seemed immune to the Goliath terror afflicting everyone else because his thoughts were fixed on God.

David saw the battle not as warfare between human forces but as "the LORD's battle." The trembling King Saul was terrified by the giant, but David's eyes were on God as he stepped out to face Goliath. "I come to you in the name of the LORD of Heaven's Armies."

"Heaven's Armies"? What was going on?

The prophet Elisha, besieged by a great army sent to seize him, told his frightened servant, "Don't be afraid! . . . There are more on our side than on theirs!" The servant's eyes were opened to an army of angels with chariots of fire.

"Don't be afraid," the angel Gabriel said to Mary, greeting her as the "favored woman" and saying she would conceive and bear a child. Other fear-not angels pronounced the same assurance to Hagar in the desert and Zechariah in the temple and the women at Jesus's tomb. To each of them the angel said,

"Fear not!" And Jesus pronounced to his disciples on a stormy lake, "Don't be afraid."

Heavenly armies. Angels. Spiritual warfare. These can bring to mind all sorts of scenarios, but one thing is clear about spiritual warfare: there is more going on than what we see on earth. When we pray, "Our Father . . . your will be done on earth, as it is in heaven," we are connecting with realities beyond our limited understanding.

GOD'S SPLENDOR AND HOLINESS

Selections from Psalm 29

Honor the Lord, you heavenly beings;
honor the Lord for his glory and strength.
Honor the Lord for the glory of his name.
Worship the Lord in the splendor of his holiness.

Your heavenly beings, Lord—are they here among us right now? Might angels come to our rescue in our troubles? Whether they are seen or unseen, we invite your heavenly beings and your holy presence into our lives.

We rejoice, Lord, in the splendor of your holiness, for in this sin-wracked world you have provided redemption for us.

The voice of the Lord echoes above the sea.
The God of glory thunders.
The Lord thunders over the mighty sea.
The voice of the Lord is powerful;
the voice of the Lord is majestic. . . .
The voice of the Lord strikes
with bolts of lightning. . . .
In his Temple everyone shouts, "Glory!"

We long, Lord, to hear your voice! Speak to our minds and hearts that we might glory in your mighty works and your care for those who suffer. Help us to listen for your voice and to respond with recognition and joy.

Have mercy on us.

Rescue us with your glorious power and grace.

DAY 3

The Wonder of God at Work

1 Samuel 17:41–47

Let's stand beside David's brothers for a moment as they watch their brash kid brother approach Goliath.

They had to be thinking, Is this kid nuts? For forty days and nights they dreaded someone taking up the giant's challenge, his getting slashed by Goliath's sword, and then their getting slaughtered as Philistines rushed their ranks. As his brothers watched the small, unarmed figure in shepherd's clothes picking up stones from the creek, their nightmare imaginations seemed about to happen.

What a fool, they must have thought. We're dead men!

As David walked toward Goliath, the towering killing machine strode forward with his shield bearer. He sneered in contempt and cursed the boy. "Come over here, and I'll give your flesh to the birds and wild animals!"

But then came David's shouts of defiance as he ran to meet the giant and felled him.

His brothers, frozen in fear, were spectators of God's miraculous power to change everything.

The Bible, of course, is full of stories of God's miraculous victories despite impossible odds. For us in these days, with threats of so many kinds, we may well long for one of those miracles. We may not be frozen in fear like David's brothers, but we're painfully aware of what could happen to us and our loved ones.

We live with anxieties because we know so much.

Yet troubles, including the many we face now, are contexts for his mighty works. What are his mighty works? We hear reports from all over the world of revivals and dramatic rescues. Yet God's mighty works also include the quiet wonders of redemption and the miracle of a small acorn becoming a mighty oak . . . and they include his peace that comes to us when we keep our minds fixed on him.

Jeremiah 33:3 puts before us a wonderful challenge: "Call to Me, and I will answer you, and show you great and mighty things." This invitation is for each of us. For some, the great and mighty things may be remarkable achievements. Others may live simple lives, with mighty things being the whispers of the Spirit and our willing responses. The Jeremiah invitation is to live as spectators to the wonders of God all around us, at work in and through us. We see this in Philippians 2, which tells us God works in us to fulfill his good purpose.

A young man with a slingshot slew the fearsome giant, but it was more than that. It was God working in David to fulfill his purposes.

The giants of evil may appear in our lives too—in our news feeds, in hospital rooms, in an addiction or an estrangement—but we have an antidote to fear. We can set our minds on things above. Both when we see God high and lifted up in glory, and when we see his myriad wonders of creation, our hearts are lifted.

John Henry Jowett urges us to count our blessings by searching every corner. He wrote, "I have found forget-me-nots on many a rutty road. I have found wild-roses behind a barricade of nettles." Jowett tells us to look for tokens of the Lord's presence "even in the dark patches of life, among [our] disappointments and defeats." He challenges us with this from a beloved hymn: "Count your blessings!"

THE GLORY AND THE COMMANDS

Selections from Psalm 19

The heavens proclaim the glory of God.
The skies display his craftsmanship.
Day after day they continue to speak;
night after night they make him known.
They speak without a sound or word;
their voice is never heard.
Yet their message has gone throughout the earth,
and their words to all the world.

God has made a home in the heavens for the sun.
It bursts forth like a radiant bridegroom after his wedding.
It rejoices like a great athlete eager to run the race.
The sun rises at one end of the heavens
and follows its course to the other end.
Nothing can hide from its heat.

Father in heaven, let me see you high and lifted up in your glory so my soul will be lifted into your presence. I call on you to show me your great and mighty things as I face the days ahead. Thank you for the great and small wonders of your creation.

The instructions of the Lord *are perfect,*
reviving the soul.
The decrees of the Lord *are trustworthy,*
making wise the simple.
The commandments of the Lord *are right,*
bringing joy to the heart.

Please teach me, Holy Spirit, and bring joy to my heart! As I think on your wisdom and commands, help me to see clearly how to obey. When I feel prone to wander, awaken your power and grace within me. Let me keep in step with you, that I might feel the joy of obeying you in the ways that bring delight.

DAY 4

Chosen to Lead

1 Samuel 17:38–40

What happens when leaders fail? Many bad, cringeworthy things. What happens when leaders succeed? Good things, often beyond expectations.

King Saul was a narcissist who failed. He was supposedly leading the nation in obedience to God, but he loved his kingly powers far more than he loved and served the Lord. When he kept hearing Goliath's shouts and threats, he lost all courage.

Saul should have been the one to rally his men, but he failed to lead.

In sharp contrast, David felt the power of living in obedience to the Spirit. His view of the fearsome giant was framed by his focus on God's greatness and promises. David acted decisively, and he led the entire army to victory.

What a remarkable thing, and what a high privilege, that we can be called by God to lead others. Whatever our roles and relationships, we are all leaders since we all influence those around us. As believers we receive Jesus's words from John 15: "You didn't choose me. I chose you. I appointed you to go and produce lasting fruit." Whether we are in a high position or no position, when we pray and get in step with his Spirit, we affect others with the practical dynamics of God's love.

The Peace Prayer gets very practical: "Lord, make me an instrument of thy peace: where there is hatred, let me sow love; where there is injury, pardon."

Theologians describe our role as that of a pipe through which flow the power and beneficence of God to others. Instead of our being the source of the good flow, it is God at work in us. David understood this. It was not the slingshot nor his precise aim. He declared the reality. It was God who gave him the victory.

FREEDOM FROM FEAR

SELECTIONS FROM PSALM 34

I will praise the LORD at all times.
I will constantly speak his praises.
I will boast only in the LORD;
let all who are helpless take heart.
Come, let us tell of the LORD's greatness;
let us exalt his name together.

Lord, there are times I do feel helpless, and I need to hear of your greatness and to sense your power. Put your praises into my heart and soul, I pray, for sometimes I do not have it within me to praise you.

Flow through me, Lord. It is your power that strengthens me to live in obedience to your Spirit, and to lead others to do the same. Make me an instrument of peace that I might show love and healing amid the many troubles around me.

I prayed to the LORD, and he answered me.
He freed me from all my fears.
Those who look to him for help will be radiant with joy;
no shadow of shame will darken their faces.
In my desperation I prayed, and the LORD listened;
he saved me from all my troubles.

Thank you, Lord, for the many ways in which you have blessed us. We look to you for help and for your salvation from our disrupting troubles.

Bring us glimpses of your glory. Let us taste the joys you promise to those who trust and obey.

DAY 5

Identity

1 Samuel 17:12–30

David's father, Jesse, had many sons, and he was likely proud of them. They were stepping up to manly responsibilities, among them training for war as soldiers. But David as the youngest was doing the equivalent of janitorial work—tending sheep. When Samuel showed up to anoint one of Jesse's sons as the new king, the father didn't even think about his youngest. Only after Samuel rejected his other seven sons did Jesse mention that, yes, he did have young David out there with the sheep.

The brothers probably rolled their eyes. And when Samuel actually chose David and anointed him as the new king, they surely stared in total disbelief.

Later, when David shows up on the battlefield with his bread and cheese, we can imagine his brothers' reactions. They are facing a fierce army and a mighty giant eager to cut them to pieces, and their cocky kid brother asks why everyone is terrified. The oldest brother demands, "What are you doing around here anyway? . . . What about those few sheep you're supposed to be taking care of? I know about your pride and deceit. You just want to see the battle!"

When your family views you with disdain, it has a profound impact. How, then, did David forge his identity in such remarkably positive ways? And how can we?

Today we hear much about issues of identity. Our experiences in families are wildly diverse, from loving to abusive, from nurturing to dysfunctional. Our ethnicities and educations vary widely. How do we experience authentic identities that empower us in our complicated, divided world?

David in Psalm 103 shared his view of God: "The LORD is like a father to his children, tender and compassionate to those who fear him."

Our identity? *We are children of our heavenly Father.*

Galatians 3 tells us, "There is no longer Jew or Gentile, slave or free, male and female. For you are all one in Christ Jesus."

Our identity? *With other believers, we are all one.*

Ephesians 5 encourages us, "Therefore be imitators of God, as beloved children. And walk in love, as Christ loved us and gave himself up for us."

Our identity? *We are beloved.*

John wrote that God so loved the world he sent his Son. When those of us with father issues and personal failures and bitter betrayals feel lost and unloved, Romans 8 assures us that "nothing can ever separate us from God's love. Neither death nor life, neither angels nor demons, neither our fears for today nor our worries about tomorrow—not even the powers of hell can separate us from God's love."

Much in our world assaults and distorts our identity as children of God. But with David, we can remind ourselves that the Lord is like a father to his children, tender and compassionate.

SING JOYFUL PRAISES

SELECTIONS FROM PSALM 5

Because of your unfailing love, I can enter
your house;
I will worship at your Temple with deepest
awe.
Lead me in the right path, O LORD,

or my enemies will conquer me.
Make your way plain for me to follow.

Father in heaven, thank you for your love for us, and thank you that I can rejoice as your child, reconciled to you through your Son. Show me today how I can truly live as your beloved child as I face the challenges before me.

Guide me in all my choices this day. Please grant me your grace to do your will.

Let all who take refuge in you rejoice;
let them sing joyful praises forever.
Spread your protection over them,
that all who love your name may be filled
with joy.
For you bless the godly, O Lord;
you surround them with your shield of love.

Thank you that you are my heavenly Father! Help me to remember that wonderful truth all through this day. Help me to walk in your presence.

Be with me, Lord, and draw me close even when I am distracted and feeling apart from you. Draw me back to your presence and enable me to show my love for you.

DAY 6

Our Giants

1 Samuel 17:48–51

When the giants of bitter things loom large in our lives, how do we view them and gain perspective? One of the secrets of David's courage and resilience in all his troubles was his praising God.

Ann Voskamp in her wondrous book *One Thousand Gifts* describes dark experiences in her life, starting with her witnessing the accidental death of her little sister. "For years of mornings," she writes, "I have woken wanting to die. . . . For years, I have pulled the covers up over my head, dreading to begin another day. . . . I wake to self-hatred . . . the restless anxiety that I am failing. Always, the failing."

Ann, a farmer's wife and homeschooling mother of six—festering with bitterness and living afraid and weary—took a dare, "a love dare of sorts." She decided to make a list of a thousand gifts for which to give thanks, gifts in her daily life. And she started:

1. Morning shadows across the old floors
2. Jam piled high on the toast
3. Cry of blue jay from high in the spruce

Ann quotes Jesus as giving thanks after breaking the bread. After eloquently describing bright colors in soap bubbles, she writes her gift number 362: "Suds . . . all color in sun."

Her giving of thanks day after day changed her perspective, dealt with the dark giants of past and present, and focused her mind on the gifts from God's hand. As we read in James 1, "Every good gift and every perfect gift is from above, coming down from the Father of lights."

Praise, which we find so often in the Psalms, delivered Ann Voskamp from her depression and despair. Researchers have long identified gratitude as the healthiest emotion. Praise and gratitude are the opposites of rage and envy that poison our bodies.

C. S. Lewis in his book on the Psalms noticed something intriguing about those who praised, "how the humblest, and at the same time most balanced and capacious, minds praised most, while the cranks, misfits and malcontents praised least." He added that "praise almost seems to be inner health made audible."

Praise has been described as profoundly transforming, and it surely was for Ann and for many others. Troubles can tower over our lives like malignant giants, but praise aligns us with God's power over evil, bitterness, and death.

In *Pilgrim's Progress*, Christian found himself in the castle of Giant Despair. Severely beaten and left for days without food or water in a dungeon, he was ready to kill himself.

"Why . . . should you choose life," the giant demanded of Christian, "seeing it is attended with so much bitterness?"

How did Christian escape Giant Despair's dungeon? He used the Promise key. Scriptural promises are many, including all those praises in the Psalms. And we find in 1 John 4 this promise: "Perfect love casts out fear."

MIGHTY ANGELS AND US

Selections from Psalm 103

Let all that I am praise the Lord;
with my whole heart, I will praise his holy name.
Let all that I am praise the Lord;

may I never forget the good things he does
for me. . . .
He fills my life with good things.
My youth is renewed like the eagle's!

Father in heaven, I do praise your holy name, and I am deeply grateful for all that you have done for me and those I love. Help me to be renewed, Lord, for I seldom feel like an eagle with restored youth. Grant me strength for all I deal with today.

When I look out my windows and see the beauty of your creation, when I walk by trees and water and see birds in flight, I praise you.

The Lord *is compassionate and merciful,*
slow to get angry and filled with unfailing
love. . . .
He does not punish us for all our sins;
he does not deal harshly with us, as we
deserve.
For his unfailing love toward those who fear
him
is as great as the height of the heavens
above the earth.
He has removed our sins as far from us
as the east is from the west.

Father in heaven, you know so well the ways in which I fail. Thank you for your compassion and your forgiveness and your great love.

You said, Jesus, we need to become like little children. I come now as a child to your Father to enjoy his love and to praise him for his wonderful works.

Praise the Lord*, you angels,*
you mighty ones who carry out his plans,

listening for each of his commands.
Yes, praise the Lord, *you armies of angels*
who serve him and do his will!
Praise the Lord, *everything he has created,*
everything in all his kingdom.

Let all that I am praise the Lord.

How delightful to think that when I praise you, Lord, I am joining armies of angels who praise you and do your will. Let me praise you and do your will this day. Grant me the presence of your Spirit that I may truly be in step with you.

DAY 7

What Have I Done?

1 Samuel 18:5–11

After killing Goliath, David was viewed as a great hero and Saul made him a commander in his army. But tormented by an evil spirit, Saul became so jealous of the younger man that he tried over and over again to kill him.

David had done nothing wrong, but he was in an impossible situation. He hadn't asked to be anointed the new king—he had been out tending sheep when Samuel came along and singled him out. And now as a victorious commander, he was not fomenting rebellion against King Saul. Quite the opposite! When he was asked to play soothing harp music for the tormented king, he did. Yet as David was playing the harp, Saul tried to spear him against the wall.

Twice Saul threw his spear at him, trying to kill him! David asked the king, "What have I done?" But Saul didn't answer, and then he ordered his son Jonathan to assassinate David. The prince asked his father the same question: "What has he done?"

Instead of backing off, King Saul ordered soldiers to watch David's house and to kill him when he came out in the morning.

David had done nothing to deserve death. He was innocent, yet evil in this fallen world does terrible things to the innocent.

David didn't simply brood about injustices against him but cried out to God, pleading for help. We see this in many of his psalms. For instance, in Psalm 7 we read,

Arise, O Lord, in anger! . . .
  Wake up, my God, and bring justice! . . .
Declare me righteous, . . .
  for I am innocent. . . .
End the evil of those who are wicked,
  and defend the righteous.

David believed God was hearing his prayers, recognizing it was God who had to do the delivering—as when he had faced Goliath. David with the five smooth stones was helpless to take down the giant on his own.

When troubles disrupt and threaten our lives, we may feel helpless. Norwegian theologian Ole Hallesby, who spent time in a Nazi concentration camp, emphasized in his book *Prayer* that "prayer is for the helpless." The truth is helplessness is a fact of the human condition, for things happen to us that we cannot control. Accepting that reality opens us to a deeper understanding of spiritual dynamics.

When we are helpless, God's promises give us hope. As Paul wrote in 2 Corinthians 12: "My grace is sufficient for you, for my power is made perfect in weakness."

WAKE UP! RESCUE ME

SELECTIONS FROM PSALM 59

A psalm of David, regarding the time Saul sent soldiers to watch David's house in order to kill him.

Rescue me from my enemies, O God.
  Protect me from those who have come to destroy me. . . .
They have set an ambush for me.
  Fierce enemies are out there waiting, LORD,

though I have not sinned or offended them.
I have done nothing wrong,
yet they prepare to attack me.
Wake up! See what is happening and help me!

Lord, I don't have a murderous king trying to kill me, but I'm keenly aware of your warnings about evil spirits warring against my soul and seeking to devour me. The longer I live, the more I realize that without your engagement in this warfare, I truly am helpless.

Deliver us from evil, Lord. Fill me and my fellow believers with an awareness of your Spirit. Guide us on your paths.

You are my strength; I wait for you to rescue me,
for you, O God, are my fortress. . . .

Each morning I will sing with joy about your unfailing love.
For you have been my refuge,
a place of safety when I am in distress.
O my Strength, to you I sing praises,
for you, O God, are my refuge,
the God who shows me unfailing love.

Here I am, Lord, in need of rescue from so much that happens around me. I pray not only for myself but for all these who call on your name and have such grave situations they struggle with.

Be our refuge and fortress and place of safety . . . and of joy. Only you can do that for us, Lord. We praise you for your promises and your love.

DAY 8

Bonding Like Jonathan

1 Samuel 20

King Saul's son Jonathan was in a soul-wrenching predicament. His father was tormented by an evil spirit. His friend David was filled with the Spirit of the Lord and had been anointed to replace his father. In that dark turmoil, many people had hard choices to make, especially the son of the king. Jonathan was torn between loyalty to his father and loyalty to David's spiritual authenticity.

Astonished at the evil in his father, the young prince put his own life in danger by protecting David. Jonathan bonded with him and they made a solemn pact of friendship.

The pact was crucial to David's survival. Jonathan refused to assassinate David. When Saul ordered him to "go and get him so I can kill him," Jonathan's refusal made the king so full of rage that he hurled his spear at his own son.

Jonathan dodged the spear and, though he was heir to the throne, resisted his father's evil plans. He did everything he could to protect his soul brother, David.

What can we learn from the deep friendship of David and Jonathan? Ecclesiastes 4:9 reminds us that "two are better than one." The bonding of these two young men in evil circumstances illustrates the need in our own distressing circumstances to bond with fellow believers.

The personal touches in Paul's letters give us wonderful illustrations of his bonding with Christians in various cities. If we peruse Paul's personal notes in his epistles, we see how strong and enriching the bonding was, embedded in his eloquent writing on love in action. To Timothy he wrote, "I constantly remember you in my prayers. Recalling your tears, I long to see you, so that I may be filled with joy."

In the first chapter of Romans, he greets all "who are loved by God." He goes on to thank God for them and adds, "God knows how often I pray for you. Day and night I bring you and your needs in prayer to God."

As we pray for one another, our bonding grows stronger. It grows also by getting together, and Paul writes that he is praying to see the believers in Rome so they can encourage each other.

The personal nuggets in Romans reveal how much these believers mean to Paul as he names person after person:

> I commend to you our sister Phoebe, who is a deacon. . . . Welcome her in the Lord as one who is worthy of honor.
>
> Give my greetings to Priscilla and Aquila. . . . They once risked their lives for me.
>
> Greet my dear friend Epenetus.
>
> Give my greetings to Mary, who has worked so hard for your benefit.

On and on it goes, naming "dear friends" and more greetings, including to "Apelles, a good man whom Christ approves," and Rufus and his mother, "who has been a mother to me."

Martin Luther King Jr. spoke often of "the Beloved Community." For Paul the churches he was writing to were indeed beloved communities. Did they have problems? Yes, serious ones, which Paul boldly addressed.

Do the churches in which we worship and have fellowship have problems? Yes, and we must address them, while at the same time giving thanks as we see in Paul's letters.

Here is his heartening farewell at the end of 2 Corinthians: "Dear brothers and sisters, I close my letter with these last words: Be joyful. Grow to maturity. Encourage each other. Live in harmony and peace. Then the God of love and peace will be with you."

THE BLESSINGS OF HARMONY

SELECTIONS FROM PSALMS 133; 138

How wonderful and pleasant it is
when brothers live together in harmony!
For harmony is as precious as the anointing oil
that was poured over Aaron's head,
that ran down his beard
and onto the border of his robe.
Harmony is as refreshing as the dew from
Mount Hermon
that falls on the mountains of Zion.
And there the LORD has pronounced his blessing,
even life everlasting.

Lord, we long for harmony! I am so grateful for my fellow believers who are soul brothers and soul sisters. But when disagreements escalate into harsh words and accusations, we know we are spoiling your life-giving harmony. Open our eyes, Father, to your perspectives. Grant us your love for those we criticize and those who judge us.

Deliver us, Lord, from lack of harmony. Let your love flow among us.

Though I am surrounded by troubles,
you will protect me from the anger of my
enemies.

You reach out your hand,
and the power of your right hand saves me.
The LORD *will work out his plans for my*
life—
for your faithful love, O LORD, *endures*
forever.
Don't abandon me, for you made me.

Yes, Lord, I do feel surrounded by troubles in this world of turmoil. Reach out to us and deliver us from evil. Show us how to respond. Enable me to be fully faithful to your working out of your plans for my life . . . and that surely includes right now!

Keep me in step with your Spirit as a positive force, sharing the harmony you give to those who call on you.

DAY 9

Ministering in Toxic Settings

1 Samuel 18:5–16

Many people now labor in toxic workplaces. We don't dodge actual spears from the boss as David did, but we may work or live where evil hangs heavy in the air.

The primal conflict of good versus evil affects us all. Some endure brutal conditions, or subtly demonic ones. Aware of it or unaware, we're all engaged in spiritual warfare.

David, despite the jealousy and hatred in the palace, was filled with the Spirit and ministered to Saul with his soothing music. Yet he was human like us, experiencing the raw emotions we see in his psalms. Like him, we who try to be instruments of God's peace may experience mixed results and decidedly mixed emotions. For many it's deeply discouraging when it seems the devil is winning in too many places and in the lives of too many people.

How do we survive spiritually and physically when we work or live in places where confusion, fear, or bitterness prevails?

David looked for guidance from God and from wise, believing counselors. In dealing with our complex challenges and choices, we need an empowering blend of spiritual and practical wisdom. The Psalms, and Proverbs, and the Gospels, and the Epistles . . . the Scriptures are full of exactly that combination. Do we remain in a job or quit? When or how do we take action to change a damaging domestic situation? Do we speak softly, or do we use a big stick? Proverbs 4 urges us to "develop good judgment. . . . Getting wisdom is the wisest thing you can do!"

Yet even wisdom is no surefire match for the evil environs we may find ourselves in. Jesus was realistic about evil in the world. He came to give us hope. "Here on earth," Jesus said, "you will have many trials and sorrows. But take heart, because I have overcome the world."

WHERE CHAOS PREVAILS

SELECTIONS FROM PSALM 11

I trust in the LORD for protection.
So why do you say to me,
"Fly like a bird to the mountains for safety!
The wicked are stringing their bows
and fitting their arrows on the bowstrings.
They shoot from the shadows
at those whose hearts are right.
The foundations of law and order have collapsed.
What can the righteous do?"

In so many ways, Lord, David's description seems true right now. So many of us live or work in places where jealousy, fear, and bitterness threaten to crush us. We ask with the psalmist, "What can the righteous do?"

In environments saturated with self-centeredness and dysfunction, we look to you, Lord, for wisdom. Please guide us, instruct us, empower us!

But the LORD is in his holy Temple;
the LORD still rules from heaven.
He watches everyone closely,
examining every person on earth.
The LORD examines both the righteous and the wicked. . . .

For the righteous LORD *loves justice.*
The virtuous will see his face.

We praise you, Father in heaven, that you love justice and are watching what is happening in our world. Thank you for loving it so much that you sent your Son to redeem us. We long for the reconciliation of all things.

Help us, Lord, to be part of your reconciliation and to love justice in all the ways you do.

DAY 10

What Jealousy Does

1 Samuel 18:6–16

Saul's jealousy is a vivid illustration of the Bible's stern warnings against it. For instance, consider Proverbs 14:30: "A heart at peace gives life to the body, but envy rots the bones."

Jealousy rotted the bones of King Saul!

Israel's king was a wreck, rotten in his tormented spirit and rotten in his actions, with devastating impacts on David and everyone dependent on him.

Proverbs 27 describes envy's devastating impact this way: "Wrath is cruel, and anger is outrageous; but who is able to stand before envy?"

Is envy really worse than cruel wrath? How could it be? Isn't envy what so many ads and commercials are selling us every day? Wouldn't envy be some shade of gray instead of stark dark?

Actually, throughout the Scriptures we see how being jealous is not simply a little flimflam personal failure. Let's face the truth about it: "Thou shalt not covet" is one of the Ten Commandments, with practical specifics. We're commanded to not covet our neighbor's house or spouse or possessions or "any thing that is thy neighbour's."

Covetousness. Jealousy. Envy. By whatever word, it's poison. James 3 describes the outcomes: "For where envying and strife is, there is confusion and every evil work."

Evil work! We see it in Saul's obsessions. Jealousy rots the bones, and it opens anyone up to the sort of downward slide Saul experienced. He was well aware of the commandment given to Moses to not covet, but he broke it anyway.

In our culture, the commandment is largely blurred. Fact is, it's been said we treat all the Ten Commandments as "the ten suggestions."

In Galatians 5 we're told the whole law can be summed up in one command, "Love your neighbor as yourself." The chapter cautions us not to envy each other, which of course we won't do if we love others as ourselves. It contrasts the wondrous fruit of the Spirit with the rotten fruit of giving in to our sinful nature, and it ends with sound advice—advice that's descriptive of the core things Saul failed to do: "Since we are living by the Spirit, let us follow the Spirit's leading in every part of our lives. Let us not become conceited, or provoke one another, or be jealous of one another."

How are we to obey the command to step back from jealousy? The counsel from Galatians is worth repeating: "Since we are living by the Spirit, let us follow the Spirit's leading in every part of our lives."

THE LORD'S REWARD

Selections from Psalm 18

A psalm of David, the servant of the Lord. He sang this song to the Lord on the day the Lord rescued him from all his enemies and from Saul. He sang:

I love you, Lord;
you are my strength.
The Lord is my rock, my fortress, and my savior;

My God is my rock, in whom I find protection.
He is my shield, the power that saves me,
and my place of safety.
I called on the Lord, who is worthy of praise,
and he saved me from my enemies.

Lord, as I call on you for protection and guidance, deliver me from envying others. Guard me from all forms of jealousy. Instead, please fill me with joy at seeing the gifting and accomplishments of others.

May your powerful creativity and light permeate my soul! Dispel envy and all that keeps me from rejoicing in you.

Save me from my enemies, both within and without.

The Lord rewarded me for doing right;
he restored me because of my innocence.
For I have kept the ways of the Lord;
I have not turned from my God to follow evil. . . .

To the faithful you show yourself faithful;
to those with integrity you show integrity.
To the pure you show yourself pure,
but to the crooked you show yourself shrewd.
You rescue the humble,
but you humiliate the proud.
You light a lamp for me.
The Lord, my God, lights up my darkness.

Thank you, heavenly Father, for the light you so often bring into my life. Help me to keep your ways this day and to turn to you as I face choices and hard challenges.

Yes, light a lamp for me, Lord. Light up our darkness. And thank you for all your love and guidance.

CONSIDER

Catastrophe brought out the best in David. In the chaos of lamentation, anger, and bitterness, with storm clouds of murder . . . we come on this wonderful line: "But David strengthened himself in the LORD his God" (1 Samuel 30:6).

—Eugene Peterson

PART TWO

The Hero, a Hunted Fugitive

You may have seen the movies—classic heart-in-your-throat sequences of a hero on the run from the government. The hero is loyal and innocent yet in the crosshairs, time after time narrowly escaping skilled assassins on the hunt. Only the hero's wits and skills keep death away. Why is the hero a fugitive? The movies slowly reveal in scene after nail-biting scene bits of the complex plot.

Why did David become a fugitive, hunted by his own government year after year after year? Unlike the action movies, this story's plot is clear. David was loyal and innocent, but King Saul's murderous jealousy never abated. He was determined to kill David, more interested in being king than in serving the God he said he served.

Those who are familiar with the stories of David may be surprised to learn how long he was a fugitive. For more than ten years Saul kept trying every way he could to hunt him down and kill him. One time Saul marshaled the entire army to hunt him; twice he recruited three thousand elite troops to do the job.

It's hard to imagine being hunted like that. David's experiences as a fugitive all those years were as harrowing as those of movie heroes escaping explosions and killer drones. One day to survive David pretended insanity, scratching on doors and drooling down his beard. He hid in caves. In the wilderness he led a band of six hundred outcasts, fighting and raiding and barely escaping.

Twice he did something utterly remarkable. When he had golden opportunities to kill Saul and change everything, he spared the murderous king's life.

David's stories are in some ways a sobering documentary of Iron Age culture and violence. A priest gives bread to David when he is starving, and Saul in retaliation murders all the priests in that town and their families. When David and his six hundred men discover their encampment destroyed and their families abducted, they track down the raiders, killing them and rescuing their women and children.

Although David's time was dramatically different from ours, the human condition of violence, ethnocentrism, and injustice continues. The unique thing about David in all that turmoil is that he kept calling on God. When we read his psalms, we get glimpses of what was surging through him.

Yet for all his God-centeredness, David was far from perfect. We love the story of David with the slingshot facing the giant, full of courage and faith, and other demonstrations of his obedience to the Spirit. Yet we wince at things he did as a fugitive and later in his life. Like all of us, he was a fallen human.

That, of course, makes his stories and psalms relevant to each of our lives today.

DAY 11

Enemies

1 Samuel 21:1–10; 22:11–23

As we meditate on David's psalms, we may be taken aback by his asking God to violently take down his enemies. It makes many a reader pause, and much has been written about that. One relevant factor to keep in mind: the depths of his enemies' treachery.

Heading the list, of course, is King Saul, who was determined to kill David despite his innocence and despite the objections of his son Jonathan. And then there was Doeg. Considering Doeg's brutalities, no wonder David wanted God to break the teeth of his enemies!

Doeg was an opportunist who toadied up to King Saul by telling him the priest Ahimelech gave bread and Goliath's sword to David. Saul, furious, had all the priests in that town arrested. Though they protested their innocence, Saul ordered all of them to be executed.

However, the soldiers knew his vile order was a violation of God's commands. They refused to kill the priests.

Saul, outraged, turned to Doeg and told him to do it. Doeg executed all eighty-five. Then he traveled to Nob, the town of the priests, and killed the priests' families—men, women, children, and babies—and all the cattle, donkeys, sheep, and goats.

Some enemy!

Evil from the pit of hell.

At Christmas we hear a similar story, of Herod's slaughter of the innocents when he ordered the murders of all the little male children and babies in Bethlehem. He did it to eliminate the Christ child . . . the child the wise men told him about . . . the holy babe they worshipped with gold, frankincense, and myrrh. We see in the story of Herod and the murdered children the horrors of evil versus the holy. We see this in the story of Saul, David, Doeg, the murdered priests, and their families.

Ephesians 6 vividly describes what goes on: "For we wrestle not against flesh and blood, but against principalities, against powers, against the rulers of the darkness of this world, against spiritual wickedness in high places." In David's world, in our world, malevolent powers drive hatreds and horrors. Rulers like Saul and henchmen like Doeg do their bidding.

David fought his battles by crying out to the Lord against his enemies. As we engage in our own spiritual warfare, so can we.

AMAZED AT EVIL STRUCK DOWN

SELECTIONS FROM PSALM 52

A psalm of David, regarding the time Doeg
the Edomite said to Saul, "David has
gone to see Ahimelech."

Why do you boast about your crimes, great
warrior?
Don't you realize God's justice continues
forever? . . .
You love evil more than good
and lies more than truth.

You love to destroy others with your words,
you liar!
But God will strike you down once and for all.

Holy Father in heaven, we long for your justice here on earth. It's hard to believe so many in our world love evil more than good and act to destroy others.

Please help us to take comfort in knowing your justice will ultimately prevail. Enable us to understand how we can effectively resist those who do evil. Teach us to be peacemakers for your sake.

The righteous will see it and be amazed.
They will laugh and say,
"Look what happens to mighty warriors
who do not trust in God.
They trust their wealth instead
and grow more and more bold in their
wickedness."

But I am like an olive tree, thriving in the
house of God.
I will always trust in God's unfailing love.
I will praise you forever, O God,
for what you have done.
I will trust in your good name
in the presence of your faithful people.

We praise you, Lord, for your grace given to the faithful who join with us in worship and in service to others. How joyous to thrive in the house of God! We are blessed that we can have fellowship with those who have received the good news of the gospel.

Help us, Lord, to internalize the assurance that despite all the evil in the world, the gospel is good news for each of us right now. Empower us to live with all the fruit of your Holy Spirit.

DAY 12

Desperation

1 Samuel 21:10–22:4

"Little rats' claws of anxiety." That's one description of what many of us feel these days in our cultural chaos. For David as a fugitive, the "rats' claws" description must have fit only too well what he felt. Day after day, year after year, his nation's military was relentlessly hunting for him. Desperate to stay alive, he had nowhere to hide.

In David's own country, anyone might have benefited from turning him in. Every move, every response to a question, could have gotten him killed. He fled to Gath, which was enemy territory. The Philistines there recalled he was honored for having slain thousands of their men in battle, so he feigned insanity and escaped to a cave.

David cried out to God for help. As we see in his psalms, he found in God a refuge.

What did that mean, and what clues might we find in his fugitive years that made that possible?

David didn't focus on himself and his needs to the exclusion of others. Instead, he welcomed his brothers and relatives and led a community of misfits.

The differences between Saul's leadership and David's are stark and instructive. For Saul, everything was about and for him. For David, everything was about God and doing the right thing. When his family and the discontented and distressed of Israel joined him, David led them wisely. He found a safe place for his parents. He inspired those with him to live by the Lord's commands. David saw beyond himself and his circumstances, which also allowed him to glimpse God's saving power.

Jim Collins in *Good to Great* identified core characteristics of the best leaders. They were not ego-driven but self-effacing. Collins called them "Level 5 leaders" and found they blended extreme personal humility with fierce resolve. He noted these effective leaders weren't "I-centric" but gave others the credit.

When Billy Graham was asked about the principles of his leadership, he immediately responded just like the Level 5 leaders. He deflected credit from himself and extended it to the Lord and to his colleagues, including Cliff Barrows and George Beverly Shea.

David was a lot more like Billy Graham than like Saul. David wasn't I-centric; he was God-centric. And he knew he could trust God, even in desperate times.

David kept asking the Lord for guidance.

When considering military action against the Philistines, he repeatedly asked the Lord what he should do . . . and then he did it. We see his prayers for guidance and help in Psalm 25:

> Show me the right path, O Lord;
> point out the road for me to follow.
> Lead me by your truth and teach me,
> for you are the God who saves me.
> All day long I put my hope in you.

In that psalm he declares that God "leads the humble in doing right, teaching them his way."

Humble leadership. Dependence on the Lord. David's attitude meant that even though he was leading a band of outlaws on the run, he could find in God a steadfast refuge.

A WALK IN GOD'S PRESENCE

Selections from Psalm 56

A psalm of David, regarding the time the Philistines seized him in Gath. . . .

O God, have mercy on me,
for people are hounding me.
My foes attack me all day long. . . .
But when I am afraid,
I will put my trust in you.
I praise God for what he has promised.
I trust in God, so why should I be afraid?
What can mere mortals do to me?

Sometimes, Lord, I feel so many things have assaulted my well-being that I can't shake off my anxieties. I do trust in you and ask that you will give me the peace you promise. Help me to keep my mind stayed on you.

Father in heaven, empower me to live with your peace in my spirit.

You keep track of all my sorrows.
You have collected all my tears in your bottle.
You have recorded each one in your book.

My enemies will retreat when I call to you for help.
This I know: God is on my side! . . .
I trust in God, so why should I be afraid?

Thank you for caring about my tears and my troubles. I know that you hear me when I cry out to you. Be with me now, Lord, and help me to rise in your strength as I face what is before me right now.

For you have rescued me from death;
you have kept my feet from slipping.
So now I can walk in your presence, O God,
in your life-giving light.

DAY 13

A Strange, True Story

1 Samuel 19:18–24

Angels and demons. Spiritual warfare. In stories and documentaries from all over the world, we get glimpses of realities beyond what we can see and hear. In the Scriptures we read of Daniel's encountering God's messengers and demonic forces, and we read of Isaiah's being overwhelmed by the otherness of God's holiness.

The Bible gives us many glimpses, and some go mostly unnoticed. That's the case with the following tale of spiritual protection soon after David escaped from Saul.

David was with Samuel in the town of Naioth. Saul found out and sent troops to capture him so he could have him killed. But when the troops arrived in Naioth, they saw Samuel leading a group of prophets who were prophesying. Instead of Saul's men arresting David, the Spirit of God came upon them and they began to prophesy too.

When Saul heard what happened, he sent more troops. Did they arrest David? No, they also joined in with Samuel and the prophets. When Saul sent a third contingent of men and they also prophesied and failed to arrest David, he decided he'd go himself and get the job done.

However, a very strange thing happened to Saul on his way to Naioth. Near the town where all this had happened, the Spirit of God came upon him and he began to prophesy too. At Naioth "he tore off his clothes and lay naked on the ground . . . prophesying in the presence of Samuel."

What a story! Even the evil in the king was swallowed up by the goodness and holiness among Samuel and David and the prophets. The story illustrates that God is greater than Satan. The holiness and love of the Lord will ultimately prevail.

Mysteries abound about good and evil in this world. Sometimes, though, God works not only in mysterious ways but in powerful, transformative ways as we see in Acts when the Holy Spirit came like "the roaring of a mighty windstorm." Flames of fire settled on each of those gathered to pray, and they were all filled with the Holy Spirit.

As we pray for God's power to prevail, we find assurance in John's words: "The Spirit who lives in you is greater than the spirit who lives in the world."

IN A PARCHED AND WEARY LAND

SELECTIONS FROM PSALM 63

A psalm of David, regarding a time David was
in the wilderness. . . .

O God, you are my God;
I earnestly search for you.
My soul thirsts for you;
my whole body longs for you
in this parched and weary land
where there is no water.
I have seen you in your sanctuary
and gazed upon your power and glory.
Your unfailing love is better than life itself;
how I praise you!
I will praise you as long as I live. . . .
I will praise you with songs of joy.

Right now, Lord, I am longing for you and a sense of your presence. I am weary from my failures and the world's disasters that defy solutions. No matter what I do or say, the troubles I'm living with and the ones I hear about sap my energies and my spiritual vitality.

I have seen you in the sanctuary and sensed your presence. As I have prayed with other believers, I have felt you are there with us. Come to me now, God. Your Spirit is greater than any force in this world. I call on you to rescue me from troubles and from my weaknesses.

I praise you, Lord, for not giving up on me.

I lie awake thinking of you,
meditating on you through the night.
Because you are my helper,
I sing for joy in the shadow of your wings.
I cling to you;
your strong right hand holds me securely.

I am secure in you, Lord, not because of my goodness or obedience but because of your unfailing love. Yes, I cling to you and will meditate on you and your promises and commandments, which are like gold—yes, fine gold.

In our dry and thirsty land, where the spirits of envy and greed prevail, and technology lures us and spreads so many dissatisfactions, I thank you for providing a refuge. I come to you in a land of angry voices ignoring your blessed reconciliation and your grace for all peoples.

Have mercy on us, Lord, in our dry and thirsty land.

DAY 14

"Revenge Is Sweet"

1 Samuel 24

Revenge movies are predictable. Early on, the bad guys destroy innocent lives in horrible ways. The enraged good guy goes after them. The scene is now set so that viewers can eventually watch with satisfaction as those horrible bad guys are thrown off cliffs or into blazing infernos or riddled by bullets.

Filmmakers know that people crave justice and that they love watching the guilty go down. "Revenge is sweet."

However, we read in Romans 12:19, "Beloved, never avenge yourselves, but leave it to the wrath of God, for it is written, 'Vengeance is mine, I will repay, says the Lord.'"

David believed that, and he did that.

Saul was determined to get rid of David, and with three thousand elite troops he set out to hunt him down. Then came a bizarre coincidence: the murderous king entered a cave to relieve himself, not knowing David and his men were hiding back in the same cave.

David's men whispered he should take the golden opportunity to kill Saul. Instead, David refused and restrained his men who were eager to kill the man who was trying to kill them.

After Saul walked out of the cave, David emerged and shouted after him, "My lord the king!"

When Saul looked around, David bowed low before him. Then David shouted that the Lord had placed Saul at his mercy in the cave, but "'I will never harm the king—he is the LORD's anointed one.' . . . I have not sinned against you, even though you have been hunting for me to kill me."

David told him, "May the LORD judge between us. Perhaps the LORD will punish you for what you are trying to do to me, but I will never harm you."

Then David added this message: "As that old proverb says, 'From evil people come evil deeds.' So you can be sure I will never harm you."

What an apt proverb! The king got the double message of David's innocence contrasted with Saul's evil deeds.

When we are personally assaulted by evil, we may find ourselves thinking variations of revenge movies' sweetly satisfying retaliations. It's so natural to side with David's men who had the obvious solution. Kill the murderous king! Yet we might ponder David's extraordinary restraint. Where did it come from?

His extraordinary focus on God!

David's quoting a proverb to Saul links to another proverb from the Bible:

> Do not rejoice when your enemy falls,
> and let not your heart be glad when he stumbles,
> lest the LORD see it and be displeased.

When we savor the punishments our enemies deserve, we get dangerously close to Saul's alliance with the evil powers. David understood that, and he personified the ancient wisdom of those two proverbs.

At the same time, David cried out to God against his enemies. His focus on God enabled him to choose righteousness over revenge.

AWAKENING THE DAWN

Selections from Psalm 57

A psalm of David, regarding the time he fled
from Saul and went into the cave. . . .

Have mercy on me, O God, have mercy!
I look to you for protection.
I will hide beneath the shadow of your wings
until the danger passes by.
I cry out to God Most High,
to God who will fulfill his purpose for
me. . . .

Be exalted, O God, above the highest heavens!
May your glory shine over all the earth.

With talk of dangers everywhere, Lord, I do cry out to you. May your will be done on earth as it is in heaven. Deliver us from evil, for thine is the kingdom, and the power, and the glory.

Yes! May it shine all over the earth.

My enemies have set a trap for me.
I am weary from distress.
They have dug a deep pit in my path,
but they themselves have fallen into it.

Vengeance is yours, Lord. Forgive us when we take delight in the fall of our political or religious enemies. In our collapsing culture, help us to stand with grace and love for those who oppose us. Enable us to stand strong while we resist the rage that is not righteous but adds fuel to flames scorching our souls.

We seek your purposes, Lord, and your ways of serving you and others. Grant us your wisdom, strength, and courage.

My heart is confident in you, O God;
my heart is confident.
No wonder I can sing your praises!
Wake up, my heart!
Wake up, O lyre and harp!
I will wake the dawn with my song. . . .
For your unfailing love is as high as the heavens.
Your faithfulness reaches to the clouds. . . .

May your glory shine over all the earth.

DAY 15

The Remarkable Woman

1 Samuel 25

In recent years much has been written about heroic and wise women of the Bible. One of these was Abigail. When she saw death threats coming her way, she averted a bloodbath by her bold and aggressive action.

In his psalms David longed for peace, but that wasn't what he was longing for when, to avenge insults from an ill-tempered, arrogant, rich man, he commanded four hundred of his men to "get your swords!" The rich man, Nabal, was Abigail's husband. Warned about what was about to happen, she sprang into action. She loaded bread, wine, meat, grain, and fruit on donkeys and sent them toward David, who was saying to his men, "May God strike me and kill me if even one man of his household is still alive tomorrow morning!"

When Abigail met up with David, she fell at his feet and begged him to listen. She admitted Nabal was a fool. She praised David because he was fighting the Lord's battles and had "not done wrong throughout [his] entire life." In an eloquent speech she predicted, "When the LORD has done all he promised and has made you leader of Israel, don't let this be a blemish on your record. Then your conscience won't have to bear the staggering burden of needless bloodshed and vengeance."

David listened, and her words completely changed his intentions. He told her, "Praise the LORD, the God of Israel, who has sent you to meet me today! Thank God for your good sense!

Bless you for keeping me from murder and from carrying out vengeance with my own hands."

Abigail was an active, effective peacemaker. Jesus said, "Blessed are the peacemakers, for they will be called children of God."

In our politicized communities, it can be difficult to be an effective peacemaker. We may be dealing with angry people with the power to crush others. Abigail understood how powerful David was, and she knew what was driving him. Spiritually they were on the same page, and that enabled her to speak to his heart.

If we are to be peacemakers, we must understand what drives the conflicts and how, perhaps, we have common commitments obscured by polarizations. As we call on God for guidance and we do what we can, we may find our humble efforts changing a mind or heart.

David viewed Abigail's intervention as God's gracious means to save him from himself. As we pray the Peace Prayer, "Lord, make me an instrument of thy peace," we place the results of our efforts in the hands of the Lord.

CLOSE TO THE BROKENHEARTED

Selections from Psalm 34

Taste and see that the Lord is good.
Oh, the joys of those who take refuge in
him! . . .

Does anyone want to live a life
that is long and prosperous?
Then keep your tongue from speaking evil
and your lips from telling lies!
Turn away from evil and do good.
Search for peace, and work to maintain it.

The eyes of the Lord watch over those who
do right;
his ears are open to their cries for help.

We long for peace, Lord! Help us to know how to be peacemakers in our bitterly divided world. We call on you to give us wisdom. Guide us by your Spirit so that we will turn away from all that displeases you.

We call on you to help us, Lord, as we try to live for you in our challenges. Show us your ways to your peace . . . and thank you for your many blessings.

The Lord hears his people when they call to
him for help. . . .
The Lord is close to the brokenhearted;
he rescues those whose spirits are crushed.

The righteous person faces many troubles,
but the Lord comes to the rescue each
time. . . .

Calamity will surely destroy the wicked. . . .
But the Lord will redeem those who serve
him.

DAY 16

David Not a Fool

1 Samuel 25

How much credit should David be given for backing off from his bloody intentions when Abigail entreated him? She was described as a beautiful woman and she was powerfully persuasive, so what man wouldn't have responded as he did? Well, consider Saul. All through these stories we have the contrast of the king who rejected plenty of good advice and acted on evil counsel, whereas David kept seeking godly wisdom.

Jesus, before describing peacemakers as blessed, said that those who "hunger and thirst after righteousness" will be filled. That describes the core of David's uniqueness. He passionately sought the counsel and the presence of God.

James 1 advises, "Everyone should be quick to listen, slow to speak and slow to become angry." David got angry at Nabal, but he was quick to listen, and he changed.

The book of Proverbs is full of practical advice, and we see in chapter 19 several nuggets of wisdom relevant to the near-tragic story of David and Abigail.

First proverb: "Sensible people control their temper; they earn respect by overlooking wrongs." David failed there.

Second proverb: "Get all the advice and instruction you can, so you will be wise the rest of your life." David listened to Abigail with sensitivity to the Spirit. As she suggested, he did not later have regrets for that day's actions.

Third proverb: "You can make many plans, but the LORD's

purpose will prevail." David acknowledged the Lord's purpose had prevailed despite his hotheadedness.

"Return home in peace," he told Abigail. "I have heard what you said. We will not kill your husband."

For us, listening to the wise with sensitivity to the Spirit can be tricky. With all the clamoring voices in our polarizing times, whom do we decide are wise?

Jesus promised his followers the Holy Spirit would teach them. Those who pray for the Spirit's guidance have a distinct edge for discernment in today's challenges and confusions. Like David, we may have to swallow hard and reverse course. Or we may find that to be faithful we must stand our ground.

When we "hunger and thirst after righteousness," we are part of God's redemption in our fallen, broken world.

DON'T LET ME FALL

SELECTIONS FROM PSALM 27

Hear me as I pray, O LORD.
Be merciful and answer me!
My heart has heard you say, "Come and talk with me."
And my heart responds, "LORD, I am coming."

Thank you, Lord, that we can come to you.

There is so much to be angry about in our world. Help us, Father, to come to you and to talk with you about how to respond and how to handle our anger.

Yes, let us talk to you.

Grant us good counsel from your Word and from your wise followers.

Teach me how to live, O LORD.
Lead me along the right path,
for my enemies are waiting for me.
Do not let me fall into their hands.

How easily, Lord, I get blindsided by the whispers from the enemy of our souls. Lead me and keep me on your path. When I am tempted to leave it, remind me of all the reasons your path is the way to all that I truly desire.

Wait patiently for the LORD.
Be brave and courageous.
Yes, wait patiently for the LORD.

DAY 17

The Persistence of Evil

1 Samuel 26

After David refused to kill him in the cave, Saul blubbered this confession: "You are a better man than I am, for you have repaid me good for evil. Yes, you have been amazingly kind to me today, for when the LORD put me in a place where you could have killed me, you didn't do it. Who else would let his enemy get away when he had him in his power? May the LORD reward you well for the kindness you have shown me today."

That was then. Did it mean Saul would back off from his evil plans? Not at all. He continued trying to kill David. When men from Ziph told him where David was hiding, he once again took three thousand elite troops with him to hunt David down.

Closing in on his prey, Saul and his men camped for the night in the wilderness. David knew where the troops had settled, and he sneaked into the camp. He located Saul sleeping near the other men, his spear stuck in the ground beside his head.

One of David's men whispered, "God has surely handed your enemy over to you this time! . . . Let me pin him to the ground with one thrust of the spear; I won't need to strike twice!"

"No!" David said. "Don't kill him. For who can remain innocent after attacking the LORD's anointed one?"

David took Saul's spear and slipped away to a hill opposite the camp. He then shouted at Saul's men, "Why haven't you guarded your master the king?"

His taunts awakened Saul, who called out, "Is that you, my son David?"

"Yes, my lord the king. Why are you chasing me? What have I done? What is my crime?"

Saul knew David was innocent. Once again Saul admitted he had sinned against him and called out, "Blessings on you, my son David." Then he promised to stop hunting him.

But David knew better. He kept thinking to himself, "Someday Saul is going to get me."

After spears thrown at him and troops sent to kill him and the king's repeated lies, David's thoughts made perfect sense. He had plenty of evidence that evil persists.

And so do we.

No matter how many laws we pass or how much education we provide, evil corrupts and shatters. To view God and evil as merely cultural constructs or figments of the imagination is to deny spiritual realities. In this world's dissonance and brokenness, we pray to our Father in heaven to not be led into temptation but delivered from evil. We believe we have a delivering Father, and we reach out to him for his love, forgiveness, empowerment, and protection from the evil one.

David believed and was empowered by the Spirit of the Lord. Year after year he felt evil's hot breath threatening his life, and he kept thinking someday Saul would get him.

But he never did.

EVIL PLANS REVERSED

Selections from Psalm 54

A psalm of David, regarding the time the
Ziphites came and said to Saul, "We
know where David is hiding." . . .

Come with great power, O God, and rescue
me!

Defend me with your might.
Listen to my prayer, O God.
Pay attention to my plea.
For strangers are attacking me;
violent people are trying to kill me.
They care nothing for God.

But God is my helper.
The Lord keeps me alive!
May the evil plans of my enemies be turned against them.

All that I am dealing with now, Lord—including those who align themselves against your will—I place in your care. Today, as in David's day, I see far too much evidence that evil persists in the world. Help me to trust in you, and after bringing all my burdens to you, to leave them there.

I pray you will enable me to "trust and obey," for I am forever learning that "there's no other way to be happy in Jesus."

Thank you, Lord, that I can come to you and leave my troubles with you. Show me, when I must make difficult decisions and conflicting voices are in my ears, how to live in harmony with your will.

I will praise your name, O Lord,
for it is good.
For you have rescued me from my troubles.

DAY 18

The Blame Game

1 Samuel 30:1–20

Disaster and great grief can cause us to turn on others for no valid reason.

David and his six hundred men, returning to their town of Ziklag, found that enemies had crushed it and burned it to the ground, carrying off their women and children. When the men saw the ruins and realized they would never again see their families, they wept . . . and continued weeping.

Then, bitter about losing their wives, sons, and daughters, they turned their anger on David. And they talked about stoning him to death.

What did David do as they talked about killing him? He "found strength in the LORD."

Can we identify with David's distress? Few of us receive death threats from family members, but harsh words and broken relationships are common. When those we love shame, criticize, or reject us, the effects are profound. When our efforts to change the dynamics fail or backfire, our pain deepens. Beyond our families and those close to us, in our caustic, wired culture we may experience personal attacks from strangers that wound us deeply.

When we experience such things, we may feel helpless.

The day David faced Goliath he wasn't helpless, but everybody thought he was. In the Ziklag ruins, grieving the loss of his abducted family, he wasn't helpless either, though some of his men thought otherwise. He could have lashed out at them, but instead of confronting them or lining up loyalists against them, he took his grief and troubles to God.

There he found comfort and empowerment.

He also found guidance. In the devastations of Ziklag he prayed to the Lord of heaven's armies. Then he rose from his prayers to lead his men to a successful rescue of their families and all their flocks and herds.

WAIT PATIENTLY

Selections from Psalm 37

Take delight in the Lord,
and he will give you your heart's desires.

Commit everything you do to the Lord.
Trust him, and he will help you.
He will make your innocence radiate like the dawn,
and the justice of your cause will shine like the noonday sun.

Be still in the presence of the Lord,
and wait patiently for him to act.

What a marvelous cycle, Lord! If I am delighted in you, then your delights are my delights, so you will give me what delights us. Thank you!

I do commit everything to you, and I call on you to help me to authentically seek justice and mercy. Let me listen all through this day for the whispers of your Spirit, and wait for you to act on my pleas for help.

Stop being angry!
Turn from your rage!

Do not lose your temper—
it only leads to harm.

Keep me, I pray, from overreacting when I feel I have very good reasons to lose my temper. Make me aware when tempers flare in a room that you are with me, that you will repay and lead and provide. Enable me to say what needs to be said without stepping away from a sense of your presence.

The LORD directs the steps of the godly.
He delights in every detail of their lives.
Though they stumble, they will never fall,
for the LORD holds them by the hand.

DAY 19

Generosity at Besor

1 Samuel 30:21–25

David, let's keep in mind, was leading a band of outlaws. His six hundred men with him were escaping something, and that number included his brothers who had always viewed him as the brash kid in the family. Conflicts were inevitable. After the near rebellion against David at Ziklag, right after the successful rescue of their families, they were at odds once again.

During the pursuit of the marauders, they had left at the brook called Besor two hundred men too exhausted to continue. They were to guard the equipment. When the four hundred who kept up the pursuit returned triumphant, some of them sneered at those who had stayed behind. "They didn't go with us, so they can't have any of the plunder we recovered. Give them their wives and children, and tell them to be gone."

David's response? "No, my brothers! Don't be selfish with what the LORD has given us."

David was "a man after God's own heart," and we see in his life various examples of generosity. That aligns with scriptural teachings. Someone intent on loving and serving God is called to be generous. First Timothy 6 tells us we should be "rich in good works and generous to those in need, always being ready to share with others."

Jesus said it is more blessed to give than to receive, and he even provided an exuberant word picture in Luke 6 to illustrate: "Give, and it will be given you. Good measure, pressed down, shaken together, running over, will be put into your lap."

The succinct counsel of Hebrews 13 is "to do good and to share." It encourages us to love each other as brothers and sisters, sharing with those in need, with strangers, with prisoners, and with the mistreated.

David was committed to God's commands and ways. He declared to his men at the brook Besor, "We share and share alike—those who go to battle and those who guard the equipment."

From then on, he made this a decree and regulation.

MADE IN GOD'S IMAGE

SELECTIONS FROM PSALMS 8; 25

O LORD, our LORD, your majestic name fills
the earth!
Your glory is higher than the heavens. . . .

When I look at the night sky and see the work
of your fingers—
the moon and the stars you set in place—
what are mere mortals that you should think
about them,
human beings that you should care for
them?
Yet you made them only a little lower than
God
and crowned them with glory and honor.
You gave them charge of everything you made,
putting all things under their authority—
the flocks and the herds
and all the wild animals,
the birds in the sky, the fish in the sea,
and everything that swims the ocean cur-
rents.

O LORD, our LORD, your majestic name fills
the earth!

Creator of all, you have given us humans so much! As you have given without measure, show us how to give to others in harmony with your will. We have so much power over animals and our planet, yet somehow our authority has resulted in damaging your creation.

Lord, we long to be wise and caring for all creation and to care for and be generous to those around us. In the complications of life in these days, we call on you to lead us.

We are mere mortals, Father, and we need your presence and your guidance.

Show me the right path, O LORD;
point out the right road for me to follow.
Lead me by your truth and teach me,
for you are the God who saves me. . . .
Remember, O LORD, your compassion and
unfailing love,
which you have shown from long ages past.

DAY 20

Bittersweet

2 Samuel 1

What did David do when he heard that Saul and Jonathan were killed on the battlefield? He composed a funeral song that included laments both for the king who had hunted him for so many years and for his son who had protected and loved him.

What a contrast between Saul and Jonathan! Their dying the same day must have generated in David churning, conflicting emotions. For most of David's adult life Saul had attempted to assassinate him. For most of his adult life Jonathan had been his soul brother. In his song David lamented, "How I weep for you, my brother Jonathan! Oh, how much I loved you!"

There's a tragic, Shakespearean aspect to this ending of a long era in David's life.

"Jesus wept."

Those two words standing alone in John's gospel have been called the greatest short story ever told. We ponder the mind-stretching implications of Jesus weeping by the grave of Lazarus whom he loved. We think also of his weeping over Jerusalem. Jesus said he had come to bring us joy, but he was also "a man of sorrows and acquainted with grief."

David. Jesus. All of humanity. When we love, we suffer loss. We read in Job 5 that we are born to sorrow, as the sparks fly upward. One of our deepest sorrows is grief.

We each experience grief in very personal ways. For instance, after the death of his beloved wife, C. S. Lewis in *A Grief*

Observed described his restlessness, tears, dread, and a "laziness" in which he "loathe[d] the slightest effort." When we lose someone beloved, we mourn, sometimes with appreciation for a life well lived and other times with turmoil, anger, or guilt.

Eugene Peterson in his book on David wrote, "Seventy percent of the Psalms are laments. These laments either originate or derive from the praying life of David. David repeatedly faced loss, disappointment, death. But he neither avoided, denied, nor soft-pedaled any of those difficulties. He faced everything and he prayed everything."

Remarkably, we can pray with this ancient, grieving king as he lamented, and we can pray with him as he pleaded and praised and expressed his wonder at God's creation and his care for us.

OUR BRIEF LIFETIMES

Selections from Psalm 39

I said to myself, "I will watch what I do
and not sin in what I say.
I will hold my tongue
when the ungodly are around me."
But as I stood there in silence—
not even speaking of good things—
the turmoil within me grew worse.
The more I thought about it,
the hotter I got,
igniting a fire of words:
"Lord, remind me how brief my time on earth
will be.
Remind me that my days are numbered—
how fleeting life is. . . .
My entire lifetime is just a moment to you;
at best, each of us is but a breath."

How strange, Lord, that our lives are so brief! How sobering to realize how fast days and years zip by! Yes, my days are numbered, and I come to you for your peace in this life and the blessed hope that afterward my days will not be numbered at all.

Thank you for the promise of eternal life with you in the presence of angels, and with all those who praise and love you.

We are merely moving shadows,
and all our busy rushing ends in nothing.
We heap up wealth,
not knowing who will spend it.
And so, LORD*, where do I put my hope?*
My only hope is in you.

Whatever happens in this life to me and those I love, all that will fade before the glories of your heaven. As I take on all the challenges before me, help me to realize that the best is yet to come.

CONSIDER

A man after God's own heart? That God saw [David] as such gives hope to us all.

—Max Lucado

PART THREE

David Reigns, Dances, Sins, and Repents

When Saul fell on the battlefield, David was thirty and his fugitive years were over. But peace was elusive. Saul loyalists proclaimed one of his sons, Ishbosheth, the new king, but the people of Judah were loyal to David. Thus began a long civil war of fierce battles, intrigue, and betrayals.

David's forces became stronger and stronger as Saul's grew weaker. Abner, a leader from Saul's side, decided to make David king over all Israel. He traveled with twenty of his men to negotiate with David, who hosted him with a feast. David then sent the rival leader on his way in safety. But Joab, one of David's leaders, violated the truce and murdered Abner.

Acting quickly to show this was not his doing, David ordered everyone to tear their clothes and mourn. He wrote a funeral song and walked behind the procession to the grave, making sure the nation knew he was not responsible for Abner's murder.

David had to deal with another treachery when two men on Saul's side figured David would reward them for getting rid of his rival. The two brothers were captains of King Ishbosheth's raiding parties, but they sneaked into his house, found him sleeping in his bed, and killed him. Then they went to David, expecting rewards. Instead, David commanded they should die because they had murdered an innocent man in his own house on his own bed.

David was a brilliant military general and led his armies to victory after victory. He was also a wise survivor of intrigue and positioned himself as leader of both sides of the civil war. Finally, after more than seven years, David was confirmed as king over all Israel.

As the now undisputed king, David consolidated his power with a long string of victories over the nation's enemies, becoming famous and powerful. He brought the ark of the covenant to Jerusalem and danced before the Lord with great joy. He made plans to build a temple for worship. He had many sons and daughters and ruled with wisdom.

But then one evening in Jerusalem, he saw a married woman named Bathsheba bathing. He summoned her, and he committed adultery with her—a crime punishable by death according to the law of Moses. That led to his attempted cover-up and the murder of her husband. Then came the prophet Nathan's accusation.

The Scriptures reveal the stories in stark detail, including David's reactions to being exposed. Later in this section we will look at Psalm 51, in which from the depths of his guilt he confesses and repents.

DAY 21

Seeking Guidance

2 Samuel 5:17–25

When the civil war finally ended and David was anointed king, the Philistines remembered what he had done to their hero Goliath, and they mobilized their forces to capture him. They spread out across a valley by his stronghold, preparing to attack, and David had big decisions to make.

As usual, he sought counsel from the Lord.

Should he go out and fight them? The Lord said, "Go ahead. I will certainly hand them over to you." David then defeated the Philistines and declared, "The LORD did it!"

Later, when the Philistines returned and again spread their troops across the valley, David asked the Lord if he should attack again. This time God's instructions were slightly different. David followed what God said, and again he struck down the Philistines encamped against him.

David was forced to make many hard decisions. Time after time he sought the Lord's guidance, time after time he succeeded, and his pattern was always to give God the credit.

As the mobilized Philistine army prepared to assault David, we can imagine what he must have felt, for we each experience challenges that threaten us. When we pray and seek guidance, will the Lord respond and give it to us? David's psalms are full of promises that God does respond. As one example, consider these excerpts from Psalm 17:

I am praying to you because I know you will answer, O God.

Show me your unfailing love in wonderful ways.

Protect me from . . . enemies who surround me.

Arise, O LORD! Stand against them.

How God responds to us and how to recognize his guidance are part of the mysteries of living by faith. Jesus said, "Keep on asking, and you will receive." What better to ask for than guidance from the Lord?

GUIDED PATHS

SELECTIONS FROM PSALM 32

Oh, what joy for those
whose disobedience is forgiven,
whose sin is put out of sight!
Yes, what joy for those
whose record the LORD has cleared of guilt,
whose lives are lived in complete honesty!

Before I can expect guidance from you, Lord, I realize I must confess all I've done to violate your command to love you first, before all things. I lay all my sins before you. Forgive me. Cleanse me.

Thank you for the freedom and joy of forgiveness.

Show me your ways to live in constant communion with you.

The LORD says, "I will guide you along the
best pathway for your life.
I will advise you and watch over you." . . .

Many sorrows come to the wicked,
but unfailing love surrounds those who trust the Lord.
So rejoice in the Lord and be glad, all you who obey him!
Shout for joy, all you whose hearts are pure!

DAY 22

Suspicions, Insults, Disaster

2 Samuel 10

A friendly king died, and David sent men with condolences. Instead of welcoming them, the new king's commanders made a huge mistake. Giving in to their suspicions, they said David's men had come as spies. Then they made rash and foolish decisions. They seized David's ambassadors and humiliated them, shaving off half their beards and cutting off half their robes.

When they finally realized how much they had angered David, they figured they'd protect themselves by hiring more than thirty thousand soldiers. But in the ensuing battles, David's men routed them all.

The defeated leaders regrouped, assembling an alliance of kings with their armies. David conquered them all, killing seven hundred charioteers and forty thousand soldiers.

The alliance surrendered and their peoples became subject to Israel.

What lessons might we take from this story? The obvious one is *don't insult the powerful.* But perhaps in our times the following three are more widely applicable.

Don't give in to suspicions.

It's not only social media that fosters suspicion and ill will. Many a bitter church split began with questioning the motives of others and making far too much of minor issues or ideologies not at the heart of the gospel. Paul dealt with plenty of that and pleaded with the Corinthians in the first chapter of his first letter: "I appeal to you, dear brothers and sisters, . . . to live in harmony with each other. Let there be no divisions in the church."

Don't be foolish.

The new king and his counselors would have been aghast if they had realized what would happen to them. Proverbs 18 describes it: "A fool's lips walk into a fight, and his mouth invites a beating."

About fools, David says this in Psalm 14: "The fool says in his heart, 'There is no God.'"

Don't humiliate.

Hazing, supposedly a fun initiation, is mostly humiliating, and it's too often deadly. So much TV humor humiliates disliked persons. It may not be deadly, but it kills the fruit of the Spirit. Love, joy, and peace don't thrive with cultural caricatures and ridicule.

We find this counsel in Isaiah 58:

> Stop pointing your finger and spreading vicious rumors!
> Feed the hungry,
> and help those in trouble.
> Then your light will shine out from the darkness,
> and the darkness around you will be as bright as noon.
> The LORD will guide you continually.

SHOW US THE WAY OF LIFE

SELECTIONS FROM PSALMS 14; 16

> *Only fools say in their hearts,*
> *"There is no God."*
> *They are corrupt, and their actions are evil;*
> *not one of them does good!*

The LORD looks down from heaven
on the entire human race;
he looks to see if anyone is truly wise,
if anyone seeks God.
But no, all have turned away;
all have become corrupt.
Not one does good,
not a single one!

I struggle with this psalm, Lord. It seems to me there are people who do good and people who are wise. At the same time, foolishness, hurtful suspicions, and humiliation are painfully common.

Folly and the human heart. Help us to understand, Lord.

Aleksandr Solzhenitsyn wrote that "the line dividing good and evil cuts through the heart of every human being," and Jeremiah said, "The heart is deceitful above all things, and desperately wicked." David wasn't the only one saying all have rejected your wisdom.

Thank you, Father in heaven, that you so loved the world you sent your Son to save us from our self-destructive folly and to reconcile us to yourself. Today, please grant us a renewed sense of your redemption and the beauty of your wisdom and holiness.

I know the LORD is always with me.
I will not be shaken, for he is right beside me.

No wonder my heart is glad, and I rejoice.
My body rests in safety.
For you will not leave my soul among the dead
or allow your holy one to rot in the grave.
You will show me the way of life,
granting me the joy of your presence
and the pleasures of living with you forever.

DAY 23

Kindness

2 Samuel 9

After David consolidated his power, he wondered if anyone in Saul's family was still alive. He asked if there was someone to whom he could show kindness for Jonathan's sake and learned Mephibosheth, Jonathan's son, had survived the wars.

When they brought Mephibosheth before David, we're not told what the younger man thought, but likely he was fearful. After all, he was Saul's grandson and part of the family that had fought a long and bloody civil war against David. Now that his grandfather's enemy was king with all the power, why was he summoned?

The grandson need not have worried. "Greetings, Mephibosheth," David said. "I intend to show kindness to you."

And great kindness he did show, restoring to Mephibosheth all that Saul and his family had owned and inviting him from then on to eat at his table in the palace. Mephibosheth thereafter lived in Jerusalem and ate regularly at the king's table.

Kindness.

Now and then, here and there, we see calls for it . . . perhaps online, or in graduation speeches, or when we hear a heartwarming story of kindness. Yet today's calls for kindness often come in the context of bitterness, rudeness, and rage. If we are to go against the currents—if we are to show kindness amid all the antagonisms—we have plenty of urgings in God's Word to keep at it. In 1 Corinthians 13 we read that love is "patient and kind," and Ephesians 4 urges us to be "kind and compassionate to one another." When we look at the fruit of the Spirit in Galatians 5, we see kindness listed after joy and peace.

Why was David able to show kindness? He viewed God as loving and kind. We see in Psalm 17 his calling on the Lord to "show Your marvelous lovingkindness" to those who take refuge in him, and in Psalm 36 he sings, "Oh, continue Your lovingkindness to those who know You."

David depended on God's kindness. In Psalm 69 he prays, "Hear me, O LORD, for Your lovingkindness is good," and in Psalm 40, "Let Your lovingkindness and Your truth continually preserve me."

If our view of God is like David's, we can emulate our heavenly Father even when we are distressed by distinctly unkind and even infuriating things that come our way.

THE JOYS OF KINDNESS

SELECTIONS FROM PSALMS 41; 17

Oh, the joys of those who are kind to the
poor!
The LORD rescues them when they are in
trouble.

Father in heaven, so often poor people in trouble aren't rescued at all! Help us, Lord, in this ocean of need we see in so many places to be kind as you are kind.

Please lift your mighty hand to rescue them!

Help us, Lord, to engage in ways that lift up those who are poor and struggling, and that preserve their dignity. Enable us to show kindness when it comes naturally, and especially when it doesn't. Work within us to give to others the benefit of the doubt, and a kind word, and a smile of genuine empathy.

Lord, it's all too clear that to do your will in all this, we need the delight of your presence. When we're dry and discouraged, pour your love into us so we can share it with others.

O Lord, *hear my plea for justice.*
Listen to my cry for help.
Pay attention to my prayer,
for it comes from honest lips. . . .
I am praying to you because I know you will
answer, O God.
Bend down and listen as I pray.
Show me your unfailing love in wonderful
ways.

DAY 24

When Love Turns to Hate

2 Samuel 6:16–23

Countless sermons, movies, and books have centered on David and Bathsheba. But David and Michal? Not so much. What are we to make of the story of his first wife's passionate love for him that changed so dramatically? She was the daughter of King Saul and loved David the young hero. She was given to him in marriage and saved her husband's life, but many years later she viewed David with contempt.

Their story is complex and heartbreaking, so full of turbulence we might imagine it as a tragic romance movie. As a movie, it would surely include these five scenes.

The wedding.

Saul promised David his daughter in marriage if he killed one hundred Philistines, though Saul hoped David would himself be killed. But David killed two hundred Philistines, so the king had to give Michal as his bride. Imagine what she felt, knowing her father with all his power was determined to kill the man she was marrying.

Assassins.

The king sent troops to surround the couple's home with instructions to kill David when he came out. "If you don't escape tonight," Michal told her new husband, "you will be dead by morning." His bride helped him escape out a window, and when troops entered her house, she said that David was sick and couldn't get out of bed.

But then her father discovered her deception and demanded

of his daughter, "Why have you betrayed me like this and let my enemy escape?"

Michal lied. "I had to," she told him. "He threatened to kill me if I didn't help him."

Marriage interrupted.

David is on the run, trying to escape her father's many attempts to kill him. He is out of Michal's life for many years, and she is given in marriage to another man.

Two husbands.

Saul is dead and David as the new king demands his wife back. Michal is taken away from her husband Palti, and the bereft man follows along behind her, weeping. Palti is finally told, "Go back home!"

Bitterness.

David leaps and dances exuberantly before the Lord, and Michal views him with contempt. She sarcastically says to him, "How distinguished the king of Israel looked today, shamelessly exposing himself to the servant girls." David's retort? "I was dancing before the Lord, who chose me above your father and all his family!"

Spousal contempt. Spousal reaction. End of marriage.

What are we to make of this story with themes relevant to our times? We're painfully familiar with love gone wrong. We've seen marital dysfunctions spiral down, down, down and end in mutual contempt—and we grieve. In our time couples aren't split up by murderous kings, yet cultural, economic, and spiritual issues tear at their love and respect. Beautiful weddings become ugly divorces, and spousal dissonance causes deep wounds in beloved children.

We know in all these situations we cannot "fix things," just as David couldn't fix the evil and violence he faced. Yet he prayed. He confessed his failures, and he pleaded for help.

David found refuge in the Lord amid tragic turbulence and broken relationships. In our circumstances—in whatever is grieving our hearts—we are also invited to find refuge . . . and to pray that God will show his wonderful works.

JUSTICE FOR HONEST HEARTS

SELECTIONS FROM PSALM 36

Your unfailing love, O LORD, is as vast as the
heavens;
your faithfulness reaches beyond the clouds.
Your righteousness is like the mighty mountains,
your justice like the ocean depths. . . .
How precious is your unfailing love, O
God!
All humanity finds shelter
in the shadow of your wings.
You feed them from the abundance of your
own house,
letting them drink from your river of de-
lights.
For you are the fountain of life,
the light by which we see.

Creator and Redeemer, we do praise you for the delights of your faithfulness and your love for us. How wonderful that, unlike humans whose love can turn to hate, your love is unfailing. No matter the brokenness we've experienced—the contempt, dysfunction, and dissonance that have made our relationships painful—you provide shelter under your wings for all who seek you.

Thank you, Lord, for your amazing grace, and for the wonders of your abundance.

Pour out your unfailing love on those who
love you;

give justice to those with honest hearts.
Don't let the proud trample me
or the wicked push me around.
Look! Those who do evil have fallen!

Lord, you deal justly with all, including the proud and the wicked who cause sorrow and shame for so many. Forgive us for the ways we too have wounded our loved ones. May we be part of your grace this day to all who suffer from broken relationships and bitter memories.

DAY 25

The Spirit's Blocks and Checks

2 Samuel 7:1–17

When David brought the ark of the covenant to Jerusalem, he exuberantly danced and praised the Lord. What joy! Later, he summoned the prophet Nathan and said, "Look, . . . I am living in a beautiful cedar palace, but the Ark of God is out there in a tent!"

Nathan replied, "Go ahead and do whatever you have in mind, for the LORD is with you."

But that night Nathan had a vision from God, who told him that one of David's descendants would be the one to build his temple. Nathan then informed David to put his grand plans on hold.

Sometimes when moving forward with positive plans, we may find our way delayed or blocked. We may, like Nathan, be checked by the Spirit. Years ago, the leaders of Christianity Today International experienced just that when they faced two large challenges.

The first was the need for much more space for their growing staff serving multiple magazines. They decided to find a larger building, yet their purchases kept falling through. Later the rise of the internet crushed countless print publications, including most of theirs. CT no longer needed more space. "We had prayed and prayed about finding larger quarters for our staff," said one leader. "If ever there was a prayer-saturated process, it was our yearslong search. But we were blocked again and again from that huge financial commitment, and providentially that kept us solvent for the tough years ahead."

The second CT challenge was succession for top leadership. After a lengthy process the board met to confirm its decision. But then came a check from the Spirit that stunned everyone. The CT board's chairman wrote, "I am still processing what happened in our meeting. I came across the following from Oswald Chambers[:] '. . . then the sudden checking by [. . .] the Holy Spirit . . . then the way of obedience to the word of God . . .'" He added, "I believe we all had a sense of being checked by the Holy Spirit. Now to discover the way of obedience."

Afterward, Christianity Today's eventual succession in "the way of obedience" resulted in years of effective leadership.

All sorts of things get blocked in our lives. We're invited to be "prayer saturated" and sensitive to what the Lord may be doing. And we're invited to listen for the whispers of the Holy Spirit, even when we find, as did David and the CT leaders, our most cherished plans checked.

FESTIVITIES AND AWESOME DEEDS

Selections from Psalm 65

What mighty praise, O God,
belongs to you in Zion.
We will fulfill our vows to you,
for you answer our prayers.
All of us must come to you.
Though we are overwhelmed by our sins,
you forgive them all.
What joy for those you choose to bring near,
those who live in your holy courts.

Grant us, Lord, greater sensitivity to the whispers of your Holy Spirit as we make choices and navigate all the complexities of our lives. We know you answer our prayers—even when it seems to us you are silent and uninvolved. We come to you, into your holy courts through the intercession of your perfect, loving Son. Help us to have the patience you have promised to those who live in harmony with your Spirit.

What festivities await us
inside your holy Temple.

You faithfully answer our prayers with awe-
some deeds,
O God our savior.
You are the hope of everyone on earth.

Thank you, Lord, for answering our prayers faithfully, in your timing and for our good. You are our hope. So many people these days live without your direction and without hope, and we pray that you will help us to share your hope in ways that honor you and bring peace and joy to others.

Have mercy, Lord, despite our sins. Have mercy on everyone, for you so loved the world you sent your Son.

DAY 26

The Shedding of Blood

1 Chronicles 28:1–7

Our world is full of war and many forms of heartbreaking violence. David's world was also violent and heartbreaking. No matter how much we may root for David's victories, it's painful to read about the horrific death and destruction the warfare brought on so many communities.

The Scriptures repeatedly tell us God is full of compassion and love. How did the Lord view all this?

David accepted Nathan's message that God did not want him to build a temple for him. What reason did God give? Because David was "a warrior and ha[d] shed much blood."

That explanation gives us a glimpse into God's concerns and his nature. It's congruent with the descriptions in the Scriptures. In James we read that the Lord is "full of compassion and mercy." In Psalm 145 David describes God this way:

> The LORD is gracious and full of compassion,
> Slow to anger and great in mercy.
> The LORD is good to all,
> And His tender mercies are over all His works.

Jesus was in constant contact with his Father who had sent him. What motivated our heavenly Father to send him? Because he "so loved the world."

If we are to be in constant contact with the Father as Jesus was, what would that mean?

Jesus said we are to act as the Father's children, and that's a steep challenge! Here is how he said it: "Love your enemies! Do good to them. Lend to them without expecting to be repaid. Then your reward from heaven will be very great, and you will truly be acting as children of the Most High, for he is kind to those who are unthankful and wicked. You must be compassionate, just as your Father is compassionate."

The old saying "the apple doesn't fall far from the tree" illustrates the fact that we often mirror what our parents are like. Jesus shows what his Father is like. If we act as his children, Jesus says, we must be compassionate.

We would act as children of our heavenly Father.

WAKING UP THE DAWN

SELECTIONS FROM PSALM 108

My heart is confident in you, O God;
no wonder I can sing your praises with all
my heart!
Wake up, lyre and harp!
I will wake the dawn with my song,
I will thank you, LORD, *among all the people.*

How wonderful that we can be confident, Lord, in your compassion and Father love. Thank you that your great compassion sent your Son to bring light into the darkness of our world. Thank you that he was in constant communion with you so that he did not have a spirit of fear but the Spirit of the beloved Son.

We praise you, Lord, that in our world with evil and hatreds, you are full of goodness and joy . . . and that you have reached out to us with your care.

I will sing your praises among the nations.
For your unfailing love is higher than the
heavens.

Your faithfulness reaches to the clouds.
Be exalted, O God, above the highest heavens.
May your glory shine over all the earth.

Now rescue your beloved people.
Answer and save us by your power.

DAY 27

David's Awe

2 Samuel 7:18–29

Nathan's night vision included God's many promises to David: "I took you from tending sheep in the pasture and selected you to be the leader of my people Israel. I have been with you wherever you have gone, and I have destroyed all your enemies before your eyes. Now I will make your name as famous as anyone who has ever lived on the earth!" The promises went on and on, including God's making the kingdom of his descendants strong.

David seemed stunned by their breadth and scope. "Who am I, O Sovereign LORD, . . . that you have brought me this far?" Full of wonder, he prayed, "What more can I say to you? You know what your servant is really like. . . . How great you are, O Sovereign LORD!"

His sense of wonder mirrors that of Mary visited by the angel and declaring in her Magnificat:

> Oh, how my soul praises the Lord.
>   How my spirit rejoices in God my Savior!
> For he took notice of his lowly servant girl,
>   and from now on all generations will call
>   me blessed.
> For the Mighty One is holy,
>   and he has done great things for me.

When we read in 1 Peter 2 that we are chosen and have been called out of darkness into God's wonderful light, we glimpse how we share in his magnificent gift of redemption. David as the kid brother from an undistinguished family was amazed at God's generosity. We may be from circumstances high or low, but when called into his marvelous light, we too stand amazed . . . even when we feel like failures, praying with David, "You know what I'm really like."

In troubles and adversities, we have hope as we worship the God of mercy and compassion. Now and in the life to come we share in that "chosenness" in which David and the Virgin Mary rejoiced. We now journey toward home, where the lights shine out from the Father's house.

We will be welcomed there. Amazing grace!

MAJESTIC SPLENDOR

Selections from Psalm 145

I will exalt you, my God and King,
and praise your name forever and ever.
I will praise you every day;
yes, I will praise you forever.
Great is the Lord! He is most worthy of praise!
No one can measure his greatness.

Let each generation tell its children of your mighty acts;
let them proclaim your power.

Praising you, Lord, is so much better than absorbing the dark, divisive things that so dominate our screens and our discourse. Fill my mind with the wonders of your redemption, your marvelous light, and your amazing generosity. Thank you that despite my weaknesses, you have chosen me, and my home will be with you forever.

Help me to praise you in thought, word, and deed.

I will meditate on your majestic, glorious
splendor
and your wonderful miracles.
Your awe-inspiring deeds will be on every
tongue;
I will proclaim your greatness. . . .

The L*ORD* *is merciful and compassionate,*
slow to get angry and filled with unfailing
love.
The L*ORD* *is good to everyone.*
He showers compassion on all his creation.
All of your works will thank you, L*ORD*,
and your faithful followers will praise you.

DAY 28

Bathsheba

2 Samuel 11

The two David stories most people recall are those of Goliath and Bathsheba. Who can forget the tale of a giant threatening to make mincemeat of a young shepherd and then falling flat on the ground, stone in forehead? And when it comes to the tale of a woman bathing with a lustful king looking on, how could Hollywood or others resist? And the Bathsheba story includes a murder and a cover-up.

David led his men into battle after battle and was always triumphant, but one spring, "when kings normally go out to war," he stayed home in Jerusalem. One day he noticed a beautiful, married woman taking a bath, and he desired her. He was king, after all, and he was now so powerful he could have anything he wanted.

He summoned Bathsheba and committed adultery with her, but then, when she became pregnant, he knew he had a problem: her husband, Uriah. To cover up his sin, David sent secret orders to his top military leader to have Uriah deserted in battle.

How did David end up committing those crimes? What was he thinking, this "man after God's own heart" who had so often called for obedience to God's commands? How could he violate his core commitments?

David made his deadly choices step-by-step . . .

He sees Bathsheba bathing.

Struck by her unusual beauty, he sends someone to find out

who she is. He's told she's Uriah's wife, but he summons her anyway, and he sleeps with her in the palace.

Truth is, this crime wasn't adultery in the sense of two guilty parties. Bathsheba had no power to refuse David's advances. Whatever may have been her responses, this was rape.

It's been said that often sin seems natural and good at the time. David had beautiful wives and concubines and was used to having his way. Who knows what rationalizations flowed through his mind as he looked at this married woman. But king or not, he knew this violated God's commands.

His acting on those rationalizations had significant consequences.

Bathsheba sends David a message: "I'm pregnant."

An old saying fits here: "Be sure that your sin will find you out."

David recalls Uriah from the battle.

He starts the cover-up. David orders Uriah home, figuring he will sleep with his wife and the baby will be thought his. But her husband, because the troops are still on the battlefield, doesn't feel he has the right to go home, so he sleeps that night at the palace entrance. Frustrated, David next invites him to dinner to get him drunk, but Uriah still won't go home to his wife while his fellow soldiers are living in tents on the battlefield.

David arranges for Uriah's murder.

Determined to cover up his deed, David ordered his commander to place Uriah at the front lines where the battle was fiercest and then to withdraw so he would be killed. Uriah and several of his comrades were then killed in battle.

As we meditate on Holy Writ's inclusion of this tragic story, we may feel deep disappointment that a man so focused on living in obedience to God would commit such sins. How do we process the severity of his fall, and what relevance does this sordid story of the rape of an innocent woman and the murder of an innocent man have for us?

A point to ponder: David's use of the Philistines as hit men to kill Uriah. That surely doesn't relate to us since we're not planning to have someone killed. Yet online hatred abounds these days. That's sobering in light of the hard truth of 1 John 3: "Whoever hates his brother is a murderer."

We're told the devil prowls about looking for those he might devour. Spiritual warfare doesn't cease after giants are slain and great victories won.

SEARCHING FOR PEACE

Selections from Psalm 34

Come, my children, and listen to me,
and I will teach you to fear the Lord.
Does anyone want to live a life
that is long and prosperous?
Then keep your tongue from speaking evil
and your lips from telling lies!
Turn away from evil and do good.
Search for peace, and work to maintain it.

How disturbing, Lord, in the context of David's sins against Bathsheba and Uriah, to read these words from a psalm written in his fugitive years. What he was teaching then was exactly what he should have been heeding on that rooftop in Jerusalem.

David as the victorious king failed to turn away from evil. Help us, Lord, to take note and remember that no matter how authentic our passion for you, no matter how often we have walked your paths, we are vulnerable to temptations.

The eyes of the Lord *watch over those who*
do right;
his ears are open to their cries for help.

But the L*ORD turns his face against those who*
do evil. . . .
The L*ORD is close to the brokenhearted;*
he rescues those whose spirits are crushed.

How ironic, Lord, these words of David from his earlier days that you are watching over those who do right. You were fully aware of his sinful acts and their impact on innocent people.

Lord, help me to realize that you are fully aware of everything, that you are the God of justice, and that you are the God of reconciliation.

DAY 29

Nathan the Storyteller

2 Samuel 12:1–12

David thought he had gotten away with murder. When a messenger told him Uriah had been killed, he responded as if he knew nothing, and after Bathsheba's mourning period for her dead husband, he brought her to the palace and made her one of his wives.

But God, mightily displeased, sent Nathan the prophet to tell David a story.

A rich man owned many sheep and cattle, and a poor man owned one little lamb that grew up with his children. The poor man loved it and cuddled it like a baby daughter. But the rich man, to serve a guest who arrived, took the poor man's lamb, killed it, and prepared it for a meal.

Hearing the story, David was furious and declared the rich man deserved to die.

Nathan then told David the point of the story: "You are that man!"

The prophet went on with God's message to David: "I anointed you king of Israel and saved you from the power of Saul. I gave you your master's house and his wives. . . . And if that had not been enough, I would have given you much, much more. Why, then, have you despised the word of the LORD and done this horrible deed?"

What was David's response? His crimes had been exposed, but he was the king, the victorious military genius, the all-powerful ruler over his people. Here we have something unusual in David's narrative, a hinge point with effects large and significant in the rest of his stories and in the psalms he wrote. He confessed and he repented.

That a reigning, powerful monarch would so candidly admit his guilt was extraordinary.

David found forgiveness. At the same time, God viewed his sins as despicable, and he had to bear the tragic consequences on his family and his kingdom. When we read Psalm 51, we see his anguish over his own treachery and the depths of his repentance.

Some of us would be shocked and perhaps insulted at the suggestion that we could do anything as offensive to God as murdering someone. Others of us would nod in agreement with those who say if we were to look at the depths of sin in the human heart, we would each see ourselves.

Whatever our thoughts and prayers, Psalm 51 invites us to the joy of forgiveness, cleansing, and "a clean heart."

REPENTANCE AND CLEANSING

Selections from Psalm 51

A psalm of David, regarding the time Nathan
the prophet came to him after David had
committed adultery with Bathsheba.

Have mercy on me, O God,
because of your unfailing love.
Because of your great compassion,
blot out the stain of my sins.
Wash me clean from my guilt.
Purify me from my sin.
For I recognize my rebellion;
it haunts me day and night.

Lord, when I stray from your paths, help me to recognize my rebellion. If I fail you in a major way, show me in stark reality how greatly that displeases you.

Help me in times of temptation. Keep me, Father, at your table spread with the good and the best.

I have done what is evil in your sight. . . .

Wash me, and I will be whiter than
snow. . . .
Create in me a clean heart, O God.
Renew a loyal spirit within me. . . .

Forgive me for shedding blood, O God who
saves;
then I will joyfully sing of your forgive-
ness. . . .

The sacrifice you desire is a broken spirit.
You will not reject a broken and repentant
heart, O God.

Have mercy on us, Lord, when we fail you.

Help us to realize the depths of your love—that you redeem all who come to you in repentance, including those who commit terrible sins.

Grant us, we pray, your grace, compassion, and clean hearts.

DAY 30

Prayers That "Don't Work"

2 Samuel 12:13–25

A boy desperately wanted to pass an important test and his grandparents were praying for him. But he didn't pass it, and he told his grandparents, "Don't pray for me anymore! It didn't work."

When prayer doesn't "work"—when we struggle with the mysteries of "unanswered" prayers—how do we match our expectations with reality?

David prayed with great intensity when the child he conceived with Uriah's wife became desperately ill. He begged God to spare the boy, going without food and lying night after night on the bare ground. But on the seventh day, the child died.

When David learned he was dead, he got up from the ground and washed, then changed his clothes and went to the tabernacle to worship the Lord.

Like many of us, David did not get the answer he longed for and begged for, but he didn't give up on God. Despite his disappointment, he rose up, and he worshipped. Devastated by his guilt, he did not turn to evil or despair. He repented, and he prayed.

Like David, when we fail God—when we find ourselves full of guilt or despair, and when hoped-for answers don't come—that's not the time to give up. Like David, when we feel God has ignored our prayers, we must rise and worship, continuing to pray.

As king, David had great power, but God was sovereign. Prayer is recognizing we are not in control. Prayer is far more than asking; it is worship. It is glorying in the beauty and wonder of the Creator's handiwork and glory, which we see in David's psalms.

Prayer is accepting God's sovereignty.

The Bible gives us many wonderful promises about prayer, and when we wonder about "results," we must realize the uniqueness of each situation and each person. God's responses to those who pray are unique: David the guilty king, the boy whose grandparents prayed he would pass a test, and each of us with our urgent concerns.

Listening to our cries is God the great Storyteller and Story Creator, the God of compassion and mercy.

In Philippians 4 we're told to "pray about everything" and not to worry but to thank the Lord for all he's done. "Tell God what you need and . . . fix your thoughts on what is true, and honorable, and right, and pure, and lovely, and admirable. Think about things that are excellent and worthy of praise."

Good things come from the Father of lights. David confessed his sins and turned from the darkness and into the light.

JOY IN THE MORNING

Selections from Psalm 30

Sing to the Lord, all you godly ones!
Praise his holy name.
For his anger lasts only a moment,
but his favor lasts a lifetime!
Weeping may last through the night,
but joy comes with the morning.

Thank you, Lord, that you hear my cries for help and that you have promised your favor and your joy in the morning. Open my eyes to see how you are at work even when my prayers seem unanswered. Keep me faithful to you, Lord, for I know that you are faithful to me.

"Hear me, Lord, and have mercy on me.
Help me, O Lord."

You have turned my mourning into joyful dancing.
You have taken away my clothes of mourning and clothed me with joy,
that I might sing praises to you and not be silent.
O Lord my God, I will give you thanks forever!

CONSIDER

The best disposition for praying is that of being desolate, forsaken, stripped of everything.

—Augustine of Hippo

PART FOUR

David Betrayed, and Hunted Again

What are we to make of the towering presence of David in the Bible? The stories and his psalms and celebrations fill page after page after page. Jerusalem is called the city of David. The blind man who sought healing called out, "Jesus, Son of David, have mercy on me!"

David as hero. David as repentant sinner. David as psalmist praising God. He was all of these, and the complexity of his many stories of troubles as messy and maddening as our own gives us much to ponder. The lessons are far from simplistic. They are more like a tragic play or a wrenching novel. We are sobered by David's sins, encouraged by his repentance, and saddened by the bitter consequences.

Nathan conveyed this judgment from God: "Why, then, have you despised the word of the LORD and done this horrible deed? For you have murdered Uriah the Hittite with the sword of the Ammonites and stolen his wife. From this time on, your family will live by the sword. . . . I will cause your own household to rebel against you."

God's dire pronouncement came true. David's daughter Tamar and his sons Amnon and Absalom and his other children—all were caught up in bitter, yearslong tragedies.

We would hope that a man so full of passion for God, who wrote psalms that have elevated millions through the centuries, would find peace in old age. Instead, he experienced desperation and devastating heartache.

Scholars speculate Psalm 55 was written about his son Absalom's and adviser Ahithophel's betrayals:

> It is not an enemy who taunts me. . . .
> Instead, it is you—my equal,
>   my companion and close friend.
> What good fellowship we once enjoyed
>   as we walked together to the house of God.

David in this psalm is overwhelmed with fear and trembling:

>   I can't stop shaking.
> Oh, that I had wings like a dove;
>   then I would fly away . . .
>   far from this wild storm of hatred.

He cries out, "Listen to my prayer, O God. Do not ignore my cry for help!"

In these worst of circumstances, David sought the Lord. Again and again throughout his life, he would rise from the depths of disaster and call on God to cleanse, guide, and protect him.

DAY 31

Family Tragedy

2 Samuel 13

David's daughter Tamar was beautiful, and her half brother Amnon fell desperately in love with her. Knowing she could not return his love, he plotted to seduce her. He pretended to be ill and asked her to cook his favorite dish and feed him. Then he demanded she come to bed with him. When Tamar refused, he raped her.

Afterward the half brother's love turned to hate. He snarled at her to get out.

Tamar, weeping, ripped her long, beautiful robe, put ashes on her head, and went to her brother Absalom, who comforted her.

Two years later Absalom murdered Amnon for what he had done to his sister. Then Absalom fled.

David mourned for his son Amnon, and as years passed, he longed to be reunited with the son who had murdered him. When Absalom did return, it set the stage for his great conspiracy against his father.

The Scriptures do not gloss over gritty, tragic realities. We see in David's stories stark realism about the human condition, the consequences of evil, and the grace of God in this "valley of tears." The prophet Nathan predicted after David's sins of rape, murder, and betrayal tore apart a family that his own family would be torn apart by rape, murder, and betrayal.

Now, thousands of years later, they still tear apart families, communities, and nations.

Some of us live in relatively safe places, while others fear violence every day. Some of us live in nurturing families full of love and mutual respect, while others experience terrible things. David's range of experiences defies easy description. Over the years he survived powerful enemies, and his anguish over Tamar, Amnon, and Absalom was intense. Yet in the worst of circumstances, when anger surged through him, he turned to focus on God.

As navigators use gyroscopes to maintain direction, so in deadly troubles David's gyroscope of awe for the Mighty One and obedience to his laws arrested his self-centeredness and reoriented his perspective. He was a sinner. He was king because God had chosen him. In his horrific troubles, his only hope was to turn in deep humility to the Lord.

PLEADING WITH GOD

SELECTIONS FROM PSALM 6

O LORD, don't rebuke me in your anger
or discipline me in your rage.
Have compassion on me, LORD, for I am weak.
Heal me, LORD, for my bones are in agony.
I am sick at heart.
How long, O LORD, until you restore me?

Return, O LORD, and rescue me.
Save me because of your unfailing love. . . .

I am worn out from sobbing.
All night I flood my bed with weeping,
drenching it with my tears.

Lord, I am not heartsick in the way David was in this psalm, but I am far from a stranger to intensely distressing things. And there are times when I wander from you and add to the suffering and heartache around me. There are times when I realize full well that you are not pleased with me.

Draw me to yourself, Lord, because of your love. Help me to place my feet on your paths, for I don't want to live without a sense of your blessing. My journey is too tough to continue without you!

With David, Lord, I pray that no matter what I've done or failed to do, you will restore me and grant me your presence and the wonder of your peace.

Go away, all you who do evil,
for the LORD has heard my weeping.
The LORD has heard my plea;
the LORD will answer my prayer.

Thank you, Lord, for the assurance that you hear my prayer, and that you will protect me against evil spiritual forces and those who cozy up to them. Please bring into our lives your miraculous power of redemption and spiritual vitality.

DAY 32

Betrayed

2 Samuel 15

Consider the differences between David and his son Absalom. When Saul kept trying to kill him, David honored that Saul was the Lord's anointed, even when David's men pleaded for permission to kill the man who had mobilized thousands of troops to kill them. In contrast, Absalom plotted regicide against his father, undeterred by his being the Lord's anointed.

Prince Absalom had a lot going for him. Described as the most handsome man in all Israel with a perfect body, he sat at Jerusalem's gates establishing personal loyalties and stirring up sedition. The king's son stole the hearts of the people, and then he sent out secret messengers to all the tribes of Israel to begin his active rebellion.

One day a messenger arrived at the palace to tell David, "All Israel has joined Absalom in a conspiracy against you!" Betrayed by his own son, David fled for his life.

As he and his followers trudged on their way to the wilderness, people stunned by the event cried loudly in sympathy. It seemed to most that his reign was over. Walking up the road to the Mount of Olives, his head was covered, his feet were bare as a sign of mourning, and he was weeping.

Betrayal! It's not uncommon in the lives we live today, including among believers. In a survey, pastors were asked if they had ever been seriously betrayed by someone close to them. Nearly half responded that they had. Spouses can feel bitterly betrayed when divorced by those they once considered soul mates. Parents whose children not only reject them but openly ridicule them and their values feel acutely the angst of family betrayal.

David's acute pain at suddenly becoming the target of his son's deadly insurrection is far beyond most of our experiences. Yet many of us have known the grief of broken relationships. We can imagine David's emotions as he wrote Psalm 3 about his flight from his son who was recruiting tens of thousands in order to kill him.

PRAYER IN THE WORST OF TROUBLES

Selections from Psalm 3

A psalm of David, regarding the time David
fled from his son Absalom.

O Lord, I have so many enemies;
so many are against me.
So many are saying,
"God will never rescue him!"

In obvious ways, Lord, I can't relate to a king on the run. But I have known the sharp sting of betrayal, when those I've loved or thought I could trust turned against me. I have known the aching grief of broken promises and broken relationships.

Lord, I can only cry to you for rescue.

But you, O Lord, are a shield around me;
you are my glory, the one who holds my
head high.
I cried out to the Lord,
and he answered me from his holy mountain.

Thank you for this illustration that when David in his desperate situation called on you, you rescued him, and he gave you the glory. When I am in my worst troubles, help me to call on you and, when you rescue me, to give you the glory.

Praise to you, Lord, for your compassion and care.

I lay down and slept,
yet I woke up in safety,
for the LORD *was watching over me.*
I am not afraid of ten thousand enemies
who surround me on every side.

Arise, O LORD*!*
Rescue me, my God!

DAY 33

Waiting on the Lord

2 Samuel 16:5–14

David's flight from Jerusalem was a great fall from power. He was the famous and God-blessed military commander who had conquered all enemies and reigned supreme in his city, but now he was desperately vulnerable, with dim hopes for survival. As he and his weary retinue dragged themselves into the village of Bahurim, a relative of Saul came out and started throwing rocks at him. "Get out of here," the man shouted. "You stole [Saul's] throne, and now . . . you will taste some of your own medicine!"

David's men were incensed. "Why should this dead dog curse my lord the king? . . . Let me go over and cut off his head!"

"No!" David ordered his men to let him curse. "Perhaps the Lord will see that I am being wronged and will bless me because of these curses." The man kept up with them as they walked, cursing and throwing stones at David and tossing dust into the air.

In calamity, David was unlike others who were quick to kill a murderous king or to cut off a tormentor's head. Whether facing Goliath or Saul or his traitorous son, David longed to know what God was thinking and how he should act in obedience to him.

In Psalm 27 David advises,

> Wait patiently for the Lord.
> Be brave and courageous.
> Yes, wait patiently for the Lord.

And in Psalm 62 he described his personal experiences:

Let all that I am wait quietly before God,
  for my hope is in him. . . .
My victory and honor come from God alone.

That didn't mean David was passive. He acted against Absalom's rebellion, directing his advisers and commanders with brilliant strategies. In times of extreme danger, he did a lot of tense waiting, but he knew how to do that.

We are called to do the same . . . in hospital waiting rooms, in courtrooms, in our own homes. We read in Isaiah 30:18: "For the Lord is a God of justice; blessed are all those who wait for him."

In that regard, David was blessed.

WAITING FOR GOD TO ACT

Selections from Psalm 62

I wait quietly before God,
  for my victory comes from him.
He alone is my rock and my salvation,
  my fortress where I will never be shaken.

So many enemies against one man—
  all of them trying to kill me.
To them I'm just a broken-down wall
  or a tottering fence.
They plan to topple me from my high position.
  They delight in telling lies about me.
They praise me to my face
  but curse me in their hearts.

Lord, how easily David could have been full of rage at Absalom and all the others who praised him yet lied and plotted behind his back. Yet he brought his reactions to you and placed himself in your hands.

I know only too well the difference between righteous anger in tune with your justice and the rage that could eat me up. When I get angry, please focus my mind on your perspective and your promises to cleanse me and bring your peace into my soul.

Let all that I am wait quietly before God,
for my hope is in him. . . .
My victory and honor come from God alone.
He is my refuge, a rock where no enemy
can reach me.
O my people, trust in him at all times.
Pour out your heart to him,
for God is our refuge. . . .

God has spoken plainly,
and I have heard it many times:
Power, O God, belongs to you;
unfailing love, O LORD, is yours.

DAY 34

Doing the Next Thing

2 Samuel 18:1–18

Absalom mobilized the army of Israel against his father and led his thousands of troops across the Jordan River. David roused himself to lead those still loyal to him, and he divided his men into three battalions.

As they prepared to go out to battle, David told his leaders he would go with them. They strongly objected. "Even if half of us die—it will make no difference to Absalom's troops; they will be looking only for you. You are worth 10,000 of us."

He accepted their advice to stay in the town.

In the great civil-war battle of Israelites against Israelites, twenty thousand men were slaughtered. Those fighting for David were victorious.

As the battle raged, David was stuck in town. How difficult those hours of "wait[ing] patiently for the LORD" must have been for him!

We who wait for God's justice so often promised in the Scriptures are a bit like David stuck in town, waiting and wondering. We may contribute to justice in some ways, and we may experience heartening moments. Yet in our world of scams, corruption, and violence, we see far too few changes. Where is God's justice? In Ephesians 6 we're given the big picture: "For we are not fighting against flesh-and-blood enemies, but against evil rulers and authorities of the unseen world, against mighty powers in this dark world, and against evil spirits in the heavenly places."

Spiritual warfare has been going on for a very long time, and we are shown some of that in one of the prophet Daniel's visions. The men with him were suddenly terrified and Daniel fell facedown on the ground. A man lifted him and said, "Don't be afraid, Daniel. Since the first day you began to pray for understanding and to humble yourself before your God, your request has been heard in heaven. I have come in answer to your prayer. But for twenty-one days the spirit prince of the kingdom of Persia blocked my way. Then Michael, one of the archangels, came to help me."

What an intriguing glimpse of what's going on! Our requests are heard in heaven. Even while we wait for the evil and injustice of this world to be conquered, great and mighty things are happening in unseen places . . .

We pray to our heavenly Father, "Your will be done, on earth as it is in heaven."

HOPE IN GOD'S MERCY

SELECTIONS FROM PSALM 31

O LORD, I have come to you for protection;
don't let me be disgraced.
Save me, for you do what is right. . . .
Pull me from the trap my enemies set for me,
for I find protection in you alone. . . .

Have mercy on me, LORD, for I am in distress.
Tears blur my eyes.
My body and soul are withering away.
I am dying from grief;
my years are shortened by sadness. . . .

Let your favor shine on your servant.
In your unfailing love, rescue me. . . .

Praise the Lord,
for he has shown me the wonders of his unfailing love.
He kept me safe when my city was under attack.
In panic I cried out,
"I am cut off from the Lord*!"*
But you heard my cry for mercy
and answered my call for help. . . .

So be strong and courageous,
all you who put your hope in the Lord*!*

Help us, Lord, to be strong and courageous as we wait patiently for you. Sometimes hope seems to disappear in the midst of our troubles, and we feel cut off from your care. But we call on you as David did! We know that even when so much is so wrong and unjust, you are sovereign and you care for us.

Father in heaven, we are weak, but you are strong.

Empower us, Lord, to live with the courage that comes from you and with the hope of your promises to those who call on you.

DAY 35

Crushing, Disorienting Grief

2 Samuel 19:1–8

After conquering Absalom's forces, David's victorious general Joab was mightily upset with his aging king. He and thousands of loyalists had rescued him from his son's rebellion. They had won by much bloodshed, but David wasn't celebrating. Devastated by the death of Absalom, he covered his face with his hands and kept crying, "O my son Absalom! O Absalom, my son, my son!"

His grief so darkened the joy of victory that his troops crept back into town. Joab confronted David. "We saved your life today and the lives of your sons, your daughters, and your wives and concubines. Yet you act like this, making us feel ashamed of ourselves. . . . Go out there and congratulate your troops."

David then went to the town gate and met with the loyalists who had saved him.

Why couldn't David stop weeping? Was it emotional collapse after the days of trauma? Was he realizing Nathan's pronouncements of his sin's consequences had just happened? Was he overwhelmed with guilt?

Eugene Peterson in *Leap over a Wall* views David as helping cause Absalom's rebellion. He contrasts him with the father in Jesus's story of the prodigal son. "What if David had been that father? What if Absalom had been allowed to sit with his father, tell the story of his affection for Tamar, his anger at Amnon, . . . and the purgatory of his exile?" But there was a "refusal to forgive, a withholding of grace, a denial of mercy."

Should David have acted like the prodigal's father? Scripture doesn't say, but it's clear the weeping king was well aware of his role in the tragedy. His guilt and suffering were enormous, and Peterson observed that David could have become "defiant and bitter and lonely. But he didn't. He became again what we now look back on as characteristically David: humble, prayerful and compassionate."

In our all-too-human condition, we are never immune from becoming crushed by "the slings and arrows of outrageous fortune." We may like David struggle with grief over our own guilt. However deep the pits of our troubles may be, when we turn to the Lord, he listens.

PRAYER WHEN CRUSHED BY GUILT

SELECTIONS FROM PSALM 38

O LORD, don't rebuke me in your anger
or discipline me in your rage!
Your arrows have struck deep,
and your blows are crushing me.
Because of your anger, my whole body is sick;
my health is broken because of my sins. . . .
I am bent over and racked with pain.
All day long I walk around filled with grief. . . .
My groans come from an anguished heart. . . .

I am on the verge of collapse,
facing constant pain.
But I confess my sins;
I am deeply sorry for what I have done. . . .
Do not abandon me, O LORD.

Do not stand at a distance, my God.
Come quickly to help me,
O Lord my savior.

With David, I confess my sins, Lord. I may not be racked with pain and on the verge of collapse, and I may not have sinned in the ways David did. But you are holy and righteous and all love, and I am not! I have sinned, sometimes unaware of my sins against others and against you.

Forgive me, Lord. Come into my mind and heart with your cleansing and your power to change everything.

Lead me into praises for your greatness and your care for us.

DAY 36

Mercy and Forgiveness

2 Samuel 19:18–23

David, his troops having put down the rebellion, started back to Jerusalem. As he was about to cross the Jordan River, the man who had cursed and thrown stones at him fell at his feet and pleaded for forgiveness. One of David's men said he should die because he cursed the Lord's anointed, but David declared, "This is not a day for execution, for today I am once again the king of Israel!"

He told the man his life would be spared.

David knew all about the need for mercy and forgiveness. It's been said God brings meaning and purpose from the ashes of our failures, and from those ashes come also celebration.

We read in 2 Samuel 22 that on the day the Lord rescued David from his enemies, he sang a song of praise. We find in it these affirmations:

> The LORD is my rock, my fortress, and my
> savior. . . .
> I called on the LORD, who is worthy of praise,
> and he saved me from my enemies. . . .
>
> Death laid a trap in my path.
> But in my distress I cried out to the LORD. . . .
>
> He rescued me from my powerful enemies. . . .
> He led me to a place of safety;
> he rescued me because he delights in me.

Why would God delight in David? Here is what he said:

> The LORD rewarded me for doing right. . . .
> For I have kept the ways of the LORD. . . .
>   I have never abandoned his decrees. . . .
>
> God's way is perfect.
>   All the LORD's promises prove true.

David was far from perfect. He gave in to temptations, and he paid heavy prices for doing so. He was not always innocent, yet he wouldn't turn against God. He sang in this song of praise after God rescued him, "I have kept the ways of the LORD; I have not turned from my God to follow evil."

He sinned grievously, but he turned back to God.

As we process all these conflicting dynamics from David's life, we might well focus on these words from his song: "O LORD, you are my lamp. The LORD lights up my darkness."

PRAISE IN THE CREATOR'S WORLD

SELECTIONS FROM PSALM 24

> *The earth is the LORD's, and everything in it.*
>   *The world and all its people belong to him.*
> *For he laid the earth's foundations on the seas*
>   *and built it on the ocean depths.*

Creator of all things, how incredible that we can pray to you—the one who has made everything and everyone we have ever known. And we do pray to you not only as Creator but as the Redeemer who loves us and is preparing a home for us. Despite our rebellion against you and the ways we've harmed your beloved creations, we turn to you again for forgiveness and restoration.

Your mercy and your righteousness are worthy of praise that resounds from earth to the highest heavens!

Open up, ancient gates!
Open up, ancient doors,
and let the King of glory enter.
Who is the King of glory?
The L*ORD, strong and mighty;*
the L*ORD, invincible in battle.*
Open up, ancient gates!
Open up, ancient doors,
and let the King of glory enter.
Who is the King of glory?
The L*ORD of Heaven's Armies—*
he is the King of glory.

DAY 37

Praise in Calamity

2 Samuel 20:1–22

People these days are quick to admit they're full of anxieties for many reasons. Many of us are experiencing hard, hard things that are challenging our lives. Sometimes it feels strange to praise God.

David lived much of his life immersed in calamities. As soon as he returned to Jerusalem after Absalom's rebellion, the king faced another insurrection by an Israelite named Sheba son of Bicri. A second civil war nearly broke out amid bloody rivalries between David's top generals.

We often see in David's psalms jarring combinations of cries from pits of despair and exuberant praises. Crying out to God, he would suddenly break out in praises to him.

How do despair and praise mix? What does David's bursting into praise in the midst of calamities tell us?

Joni Eareckson Tada, after a diving accident at age seventeen left her with quadriplegia, was in a pit of despair. She longed to escape the pain and hopelessness and tried to find a way to commit suicide. When a friend suggested she praise the Lord, she scoffed. How could she praise God in her horrific calamity?

Yet she changed her mind. She started to praise God, and that started her on the road to vibrant faith and remarkable ministries.

David's prayer life is opened to us with his cries for deliverance, with pleas for help, and with robust exclamations of praise.

Praise? How can we praise in the context of violence, betrayal, and injustice all around us? This from Rainer Maria Rilke speaks to the paradox:

> "O tell me, poet, what do you do?"
> —I praise.
> "But how can you endure to meet the gaze
> Of deathly and of monstrous things?"
> —I praise.

David, no matter what calamity he faced, praised God. His pattern might be summarized like this: *praise in calamity; pick up stones.*

No matter how dire the threats against us, while viewing our giants we can praise God and pick up the stones he provides.

It has been said prayer should start with praise. When we see God high and lifted up and full of love for us, we are able to seek his invigorating guidance—to open ourselves to the presence of his Spirit—as we gather what we need for resilience and effectiveness in the calamity du jour.

FROM MUD AND MIRE TO JOY

SELECTIONS FROM PSALM 40

I waited patiently for the LORD to help me,
and he turned to me and heard my cry.
He lifted me out of the pit of despair,
out of the mud and the mire.
He set my feet on solid ground
and steadied me as I walked along.
He has given me a new song to sing,
a hymn of praise to our God.
Many will see what he has done and be amazed.
They will put their trust in the LORD.

How wonderful, Lord, that you do bring new songs to our hearts. You have done wonderful things among us, and we praise you for lifting us to new hope, for you are Immanuel, God with us.

Thank you for being with us! And thank you for guiding us in these troubled times.

Oh, the joys of those who trust the LORD. . . .
Your plans for us are too numerous to list. . . .
If I tried to recite all your wonderful deeds,
I would never come to the end of them. . . .

But may all who search for you
be filled with joy and gladness in you.
May those who love your salvation
repeatedly shout, "The LORD is great!"

DAY 38

Innocent, Guilty, Empowered

2 Samuel 21:1–14

A recurrent theme in David's psalms is his crying out to God for protection because of his innocence. And innocent he often was, though countless plots and attempted assassinations threatened his survival. In one account from the end of his reign, David went to the Lord during a painful three-year famine and learned that Israel was suffering not as a result of David's sins but as a consequence of Saul's sins before him.

In Psalm 17 David prays,

> O LORD, hear my plea for justice. . . .
> Pay attention to my prayer,
> for it comes from honest lips.
> Declare me innocent,
> for you see those who do right. . . .
>
> I have followed your commands,
> which keep me from following cruel and
> evil people.

Yet in Psalm 143 he calls out,

> Hear my prayer, O LORD;
> listen to my plea! . . .
> Don't put your servant on trial,
> for no one is innocent before you.

Innocent, but no one is innocent? How do we reconcile these two declarations in his psalms?

That's a question relevant not only to David's life but to the lives of all believers. We may be innocent in many ways, as David was in that he obeyed the laws of Moses and kept seeking God's guidance. We may be serving the Lord in obedience to what we see in his Word and as we listen for the whispers of his Spirit. Yet we read in 1 John 1:8, "If we claim we have no sin, we are only fooling ourselves and not living in the truth."

David did not deceive himself. He was innocent in many of the troubles he faced, but he knew he was not holy as God is holy. He needed cleansing from the Mighty One. First John 1:9 completes the innocent-guilty paradox with what happens when we confess our sins to God: "He is faithful and just to forgive us our sins and to cleanse us from all wickedness."

Through all the psalms, through all the stories, David was God-focused. We see this in Psalm 16:

> I said to the Lord, "You are my Master!
> Every good thing I have comes from
> you." . . .
>
> I will bless the Lord who guides me. . . .
> I know the Lord is always with me.

– BETTER THAN GOLD, SWEETER THAN HONEY –

Selections from Psalm 19

> *The commands of the Lord are clear,*
> *giving insight for living.*
> *Reverence for the Lord is pure,*
> *lasting forever.*
> *The laws of the Lord are true;*
> *each one is fair.*

They are more desirable than gold,
even the finest gold.
They are sweeter than honey,
even honey dripping from the comb.
They are a warning to your servant,
a great reward for those who obey them.

In these confusing, chaotic times, Lord, how wonderful to have your insights for living, your laws and promises that truly are more valuable than gold. I love the truths of your Word. Stashes of money or even piles of gold coins under my bed would mean little if I'm living in destructive ways that produce misery.

Thank you for giving us your pure gold! Empower us to respond with gratitude as we learn your ways, confess our sins, and walk in step with your Holy Spirit.

How can I know all the sins lurking in my heart?
Cleanse me from these hidden faults.
Keep your servant from deliberate sins!
Don't let them control me.
Then I will be free of guilt
and innocent of great sin.

May the words of my mouth
and the meditation of my heart
be pleasing to you,
O Lord*, my rock and my redeemer.*

DAY 39

Last Words: Passing the Torch

1 Kings 2:1–4

David had chosen his son Solomon as his successor. As his time of death approached, he charged the soon-to-be new king, "Take courage and be a man."

Be a man? In our culture today, that charge would generate both heat and light, objections and affirmations! What does it mean to be a man? Well, we all need courage, men and women, and whatever the cultural dynamics, we all need to step up to our responsibilities. David's next words to young Solomon sum up our mandate as believers: "Observe the requirements of the LORD your God, and follow all his ways."

Among David's last recorded words is his acknowledgment of the source of his psalms. "The Spirit of the LORD speaks through me; his words are upon my tongue." He added that God had said to him about leadership,

> The one who rules righteously,
>   who rules in the fear of God,
> is like the light of morning at sunrise,
>   like a morning without clouds,
> like the gleaming of the sun
>   on new grass after rain.

The deep desire of David's heart was to be exactly that kind of king, ruling righteously in the fear of God. As the "sweet psalmist" he expressed in those last words the result of such rule with images of the beauty of God's creation.

REJOICING IN GOD'S GUIDANCE

SELECTIONS FROM PSALM 16

Keep me safe, O God,
for I have come to you for refuge. . . .

LORD, you alone are my inheritance, my cup of blessing.
You guard all that is mine. . . .

I will bless the LORD who guides me;
even at night my heart instructs me.
I know the LORD is always with me.
I will not be shaken, for he is right beside me.

It's wonderful, Lord, when I sense that you are beside me and that whatever I am doing, you are there with me to guide and bless. Please give me courage to meet my responsibilities and lead righteously wherever you have given me influence. Where I need to pass on opportunity and authority, teach me to do so in the fear of the Lord.

Heavenly Father, help me not to be shaken today but to live now and forever as your beloved child.

No wonder my heart is glad, and I rejoice. . . .
For you will not leave my soul among the dead
or allow your holy one to rot in the grave.
You will show me the way of life,
granting me the joy of your presence
and the pleasures of living with you forever.

DAY 40

David's Shepherd

Psalm 23

Psalm 23 has been called the most loved passage in all the Bible and a source of comfort to millions who have memorized it. We are drawn to familiar words profound in their simplicity:

The Lord is my shepherd.

That's a joyous declaration, a big cause to celebrate! Our God of mercy and compassion leads and protects. And Jesus said, "I am the good shepherd. . . . I lay down my life for the sheep."

I have all that I need.

We are in the Good Shepherd's care and so we can be content. Whatever our circumstances, as Paul wrote in 1 Timothy 6, "Godliness with contentment is great gain."

He leads me beside peaceful streams.

From the cacophony of our culture's bitter accusations, our Shepherd leads us to streams of his love and peace. We see in his creation wonders and beauty, and in the believing community glimpses of the authentic peace we all long for.

He guides me.

Today's freedoms enable many of us to make unlimited choices—and we desperately need wisdom and guidance. Isaiah 53 says that we all like sheep have gone astray and turned to our own ways. But God's paths of righteousness make possible green pastures and still waters that restore the soul.

Through the darkest valley, I will not be afraid.

You've likely heard Woody Guthrie's lyrics, "You gotta walk

that lonesome valley, you gotta walk it by yourself." But even in the nearness of death, we are not alone. The Shepherd walks beside us. He is with us. We need not fear.

My cup overflows with blessings.

When we focus on God, we see more clearly the blessings in our lives. Sometimes we simply need to recognize and celebrate them.

Unfailing love will pursue me.

What an encouraging promise! Even when I stray, even when I am tempted to wander, the Shepherd not only pursues me but pursues me with his love. And he will be doing this for the rest of my life!

I will live in the house of the Lord *forever.*

Jesus, the Good Shepherd, told his disciples, "My Father's house has many rooms. . . . I am going there to prepare a place for you."

We find fascinating glimpses of his Father's house in the book of Revelation. "He will wipe every tear from their eyes, and there will be no more death or sorrow or crying or pain." An angel showed the apostle John a river with the water of life, clear as crystal, with a tree of life on each side. "No longer will there be a curse upon anything."

No wonder heaven is called "a far better place."

Deep, deep within all of us, we long for the home of our heavenly Father. Hebrews 11 observes that we're "strangers on earth . . . longing for a better country—a heavenly one." At Christmas we hear songs of traveling home for the holidays to be with those we love. Heaven is heavenly because God is love and we will be with him. As the song goes, "The love of God is greater far than tongue or pen can ever tell."

In Jesus's story of the prodigal son, the waiting father joyously celebrates when his son comes home. Jesus said he had come that we might have joy, and that our joy might be full. Heaven is a place of joy.

Psalm 23 concludes, "I will live in the house of the LORD forever." We will be home with our heavenly Father who loves us.

DAVID'S PRAYER, OUR PRAYER

PSALM 23

The LORD is my shepherd;
I have all that I need.
He lets me rest in green meadows;
he leads me beside peaceful streams.
He renews my strength.
He guides me along right paths,
bringing honor to his name.

Lord, thank you for your loving care and guidance. Help me to keep my feet on your paths, for I know those are the ones that enable me to walk beside green meadows and peaceful streams.

Be with me, I pray, in hard and frightening times.

Even when I walk
through the darkest valley,
I will not be afraid,
for you are close beside me.
Your rod and your staff
protect and comfort me.
You prepare a feast for me
in the presence of my enemies.
You honor me by anointing my head with oil.
My cup overflows with blessings.
Surely your goodness and unfailing love will
pursue me
all the days of my life,
and I will live in the house of the LORD
forever.

APPENDIX

Courage and Resilience from Heaven

Everyone experiences fear, and throughout the Bible we find songs, stories, wise sayings, encouragements, and challenges relevant to our fears and anxieties. For your easy reference I have provided below a few selections.

David, like all of us, felt fear, but he brought his fears to the Lord. From the breadth of the Scriptures, we gain insights into God's love for us and his invitation to call on him in times of trouble.

The verses below start with a few of the Bible's many angel appearances. The King James Version translated the angel assurances as "Fear not," and more modern translations read "Don't be afraid."

Fear. It's a response that keeps us alive when we're dodging a careening truck or responding to a fire alarm. But fear can be paralyzing, and as a bundle of dreads and anxieties, it's destructive.

What do the Scriptures mean when they urge us not to fear? I invite you to meditate on the passages below and to read the full context of these brief samplings.

"Fear-Not" Angels

Daniel 8:15–17; 10:17–19

As I, Daniel, was trying to understand the meaning of this vision, someone who looked like a man stood in front of me. And I heard a human voice calling out from the Ulai River, "Gabriel, tell this man the meaning of his vision."

As Gabriel approached the place where I was standing, I became so terrified that I fell with my face to the ground. . . .

"How can someone like me, your servant, talk to you, my lord? My strength is gone, and I can hardly breathe."

Then the one who looked like a man touched me again, and I felt my strength returning. "Don't be afraid," he said, "for you are very precious to God. Peace! Be encouraged! Be strong!"

Matthew 1:18–21 ESV

Now the birth of Jesus Christ took place in this way. When his mother Mary had been betrothed to Joseph, before they came together she was found to be with child from the Holy Spirit. And her husband Joseph, being a just man and unwilling to put her to shame, resolved to divorce her quietly. But as he considered these things, behold, an angel of the Lord appeared to him in a dream, saying, "Joseph, son of David, do not fear to take Mary as your wife, for that which is conceived in her is from the Holy Spirit. She will bear a son, and you shall call his name Jesus, for he will save his people from their sins."

Matthew 28:1–6 NKJV

Now after the Sabbath, as the first day of the week began to dawn, Mary Magdalene and the other Mary came to see the tomb. And behold, there was a great earthquake; for an angel of the Lord descended from heaven, and came and rolled back the stone from the door, and sat on it. His countenance was like lightning, and his clothing as white as snow. And the guards shook for fear of him, and became like dead men.

But the angel answered and said to the women, "Do not be afraid, for I know that you seek Jesus who was crucified. He is not here; for He is risen, as He said."

LUKE 1:11–15 ESV

And there appeared to him an angel of the Lord standing on the right side of the altar of incense. And Zechariah was troubled when he saw him, and fear fell upon him. But the angel said to him, "Do not be afraid, Zechariah, for your prayer has been heard, and your wife Elizabeth will bear you a son, and you shall call his name John. And you will have joy and gladness, and many will rejoice at his birth, for he will be great before the Lord."

LUKE 1:26–31 NIV

In the sixth month of Elizabeth's pregnancy, God sent the angel Gabriel to Nazareth, a town in Galilee, to a virgin pledged to be married to a man named Joseph, a descendant of David. The virgin's name was Mary. The angel went to her and said, "Greetings, you who are highly favored! The Lord is with you."

Mary was greatly troubled at his words and wondered what kind of greeting this might be. But the angel said to her, "Do not be afraid, Mary; you have found favor with God. You will conceive and give birth to a son, and you are to call him Jesus."

LUKE 2:8–11 NKJV

Now there were in the same country shepherds living out in the fields, keeping watch over their flock by night. And behold, an angel of the Lord stood before them, and the glory of the Lord shone around them, and they were greatly afraid. Then the angel said to them, "Do not be afraid, for behold, I bring you good tidings of great joy which will be to all people. For there is born to you this day in the city of David a Savior, who is Christ the Lord."

Encouragements for Early Christians

ROMANS 8:15–16, 38–39 ESV

For you did not receive the spirit of slavery to fall back into fear, but you have received the Spirit of adoption as sons, by whom we cry, "Abba! Father!" The Spirit himself bears witness with our spirit that we are children of God. . . .

For I am sure that neither death nor life, nor angels nor rulers, nor things present nor things to come, nor powers, nor height nor depth, nor anything else in all of creation, will be able to separate us from the love of God in Christ Jesus our Lord.

PHILIPPIANS 4:6–7 NIV

Do not be anxious about anything, but in every situation, by prayer and petition, with thanksgiving, present your requests to God. And the peace of God, which transcends all understanding, will guard your hearts and your minds in Christ Jesus.

2 TIMOTHY 1:7 NKJV

For God has not given us a spirit of fear, but of power and of love and of a sound mind.

HEBREWS 13:5–6 ESV

Keep your life free from love of money, and be content with what you have, for he has said, "I will never leave you nor forsake you." So we can confidently say,

> "The Lord is my helper;
>   I will not fear;
> What can man do to me?"

1 Peter 5:6–7 NIV

Humble yourselves, therefore, under God's mighty hand, that he may lift you up in due time. Cast all your anxiety on him because he cares for you.

David's Fears and Courage

Psalm 5:11–12 ESV

But let all who take refuge in you rejoice;
  let them ever sing for joy,
and spread your protection over them,
  that those who love your name may exult
    in you.
For you bless the righteous, O Lord;
  you cover him with favor as with a shield.

Psalm 23:4 NIV

Even though I walk
  through the darkest valley,
I will fear no evil,
  for you are with me.

Psalm 27:1, 14 NKJV

The Lord is my light and my salvation;
Whom shall I fear? . . .
Wait on the Lord;
Be of good courage,
And He shall strengthen your heart;
Wait, I say, on the Lord!

Psalm 34:4–5 ESV

I sought the Lord, and he answered me
and delivered me from all my fears.
Those who look to him are radiant,
and their faces shall never be ashamed.

Psalm 56:3–4 NIV

When I am afraid, I put my trust in you.
In God, whose word I praise—
in God I trust and am not afraid.
What can mere mortals do to me?

Jesus on Fear and Anxiety

Matthew 10:28–31 NKJV

Do not fear those who kill the body but cannot kill the soul. But rather fear Him who is able to destroy both soul and body in hell. Are not two sparrows sold for a copper coin? And not one of them falls to the ground apart from your Father's will. But the very hairs of your head are all numbered. Do not fear therefore; you are of more value than many sparrows.

Mark 6:47–50 NIV

Later that night, the boat was in the middle of the lake, and [Jesus] was alone on land. He saw the disciples straining at the oars, because the wind was against them. Shortly before dawn he went out to them, walking on the lake. He was about to pass by them, but when they saw him walking on the lake, they thought he was a ghost. They cried out, because they all saw him and were terrified.

Immediately he spoke to them and said, "Take courage. It is I. Don't be afraid."

LUKE 12:29–32 ESV

And do not seek what you are to eat and what you are to drink, nor be worried. For all the nations of the world seek after these things, and your Father knows that you need them. Instead, seek his kingdom, and these things will be added to you.

Fear not, little flock, for it is your Father's good pleasure to give you the kingdom.

JOHN 14:1, 27 NKJV

Let not your heart be troubled; you believe in God, believe also in Me. . . .

Peace I leave with you, My peace I give to you; not as the world gives do I give to you. Let not your heart be troubled, neither let it be afraid.

Courage in Deep Troubles

PSALM 46:1–2 ESV

God is our refuge and strength,
a very present help in trouble.
Therefore we will not fear though the earth
gives way,
though the mountains be moved into the
heart of the sea.

ISAIAH 41:10 NIV

So do not fear, for I am with you;
do not be dismayed, for I am your God.
I will strengthen you and help you;
I will uphold you with my righteous right
hand.

Lamentations 3:52–57 ESV

I have been hunted like a bird
by those who were my enemies without
cause;
they flung me alive into the pit
and cast stones on me;
water closed over my head;
I said, "I am lost."

I called on your name, O Lord,
from the depths of the pit;
you heard my plea, "Do not close
your ear to my cry for help!"
You came near when I called on you;
you said, "Do not fear!"

Zephaniah 3:17 NIV

The Lord your God is with you,
the Mighty Warrior who saves.
He will take great delight in you;
in his love he will no longer rebuke you,
but will rejoice over you with singing.

Notes

Consider Tim Stafford, *David and David's Son: 13 Meditations on Success and Failure* (self-pub., Franklin Park Press, 2021), 30.

Day 3 **John Henry Jowett urges us:** John Henry Jowett, *My Daily Meditation for the Circling Year* (New York: Fleming H. Revell Company, 1914), 6.

Day 4 **Peace Prayer:** "Belle prière à faire pendant la messe," *La Clochette* 12 (December 1912), 285.

Day 6 **Ann Voskamp in her wondrous book:** Ann Voskamp, *One Thousand Gifts: A Dare to Live Fully Right Where You Are* (Grand Rapids, MI: Zondervan, 2011), 26–27, 44–45, 64.

C. S. Lewis in his book on the Psalms: C. S. Lewis, *Reflections on the Psalms* (New York: Harcourt, Brace, 1958), 94.

In *Pilgrim's Progress*: John Bunyan, *The Pilgrim's Progress* (London: Hurst, Robinson & Co, 1820), 136. First published 1678.

Day 7 **Norwegian theologian Ole Hallesby:** Ole Hallesby, *Prayer* (Minneapolis, MN: Augsburg Fortress, 1975), 19. First published 1931.

Consider Eugene Peterson, *Leap over a Wall: Earthy Spirituality for Everyday Christians* (San Francisco: HarperSanFrancisco, 1997), 105.

Day 12 **"Little rats' claws of anxiety":** Rosemary Budd, *Journey of Prayer* (Nashville: Upper Room Books, 1989), 179.

Jim Collins: Jim Collins, *Good to Great: Why Some Companies Make the Leap . . . And Others Don't* (New York: HarperCollins, 2011), 12–13.

Day 20 **After the death of his beloved wife:** C. S. Lewis, *A Grief Observed* (New York: HarperCollins, 2001), 5. First published 1961.

Eugene Peterson in his book on David: Eugene Peterson, *Leap over a Wall: Earthy Spirituality for Everyday Christians* (San Francisco: HarperSanFrancisco, 1997), 115.

Consider Max Lucado, *Facing Your Giants: God Still Does the Impossible* (Nashville: Thomas Nelson, 2006), 7.

Day 22 **Aleksandr Solzhenitsyn wrote:** Aleksandr Solzhenitsyn, *The Gulag Archipelago, 1918–1956: An Experiment in Literary Investigation*, vol. 1 (New York: Harper & Row, 1974), 168.

Day 25 **I came across the following from Oswald Chambers:** Oswald Chambers, *My Utmost for His Highest* (Grand Rapids, MI: Our Daily Bread Publishing, 2017), 282. First published 1927.

Consider Andrew Knowles, *Discovering Prayer* (Oxford, England: Lion Publishing, 1985), 54.

Day 35 **Eugene Peterson:** Eugene Peterson, *Leap over a Wall: Earthy Spirituality for Everyday Christians* (San Francisco: HarperSanFrancisco, 1997), 197–98.

"The slings and arrows of outrageous fortune": William Shakespeare, *Hamlet*, ed. Barbara A. Mowat and Paul Werstine (New York: Simon & Schuster, 2012), 127.

Day 37 **This from Rainer Maria Rilke:** Rainer Maria Rilke, "Oh sage, Dichter, was du tust?" December 1921.

Day 40 **Woody Guthrie's lyrics:** Woody Guthrie, "Lonesome Valley," © 1963 (renewed) and 1977 (renewed) by Woody Guthrie Publications, Inc. and TRO-Ludlow Music, Inc. (BMI).

Help us get the word out!

Our Daily Bread Publishing exists to feed the soul with the Word of God.

If you appreciated this book, please let others know.

- Pick up another copy to give as a gift.
- Share a link to the book or mention it on social media.
- Write a review on your blog, on a book-seller's website, or at our own site (odb.org/store).
- Recommend this book for your church, book club, or small group.

Connect with us:

@ourdailybread

@ourdailybread

@ourdailybread

Our Daily Bread Publishing
PO Box 3566
Grand Rapids, Michigan 49501 USA

books@odb.org